Advanced Pathfinder 2
Developing learning strategies

| Term-time opening

Other titles in the series

Tests and targets (APF3)
Ted Neather with Sophie Stringer-Lamarre

Advancing with oral work (APF1)
Anneli McLachlan

Centre for Information
on Language Teaching and Research

The Centre for Information on Language Teaching and
Research provides a complete range of services for
language professionals in every stage and sector of
education, and in business, in support of its brief to
promote Britain's foreign language capability.

CILT is a registered charity, supported by Central
Government grants. CILT is based in Covent Garden,
London, and its services are delivered through a
national collaborative network of regional Comenius
Centres in England, the National Comenius Centre of
Wales, Scottish CILT and Northern Ireland CILT.

advAnced

Pathfinder

2

Developing
learning strategies

BARRY JONES

WITH ICT CONTRIBUTIONS BY ROS WALKER

CiLT

Centre for Information
on Language Teaching and Research

The views expressed in this publication are the authors' and do not necessarily represent those of CILT.

The author and publisher would like to acknowledge the following for permission to reproduce copyright material: p12 Julia Whyte, French teacher, (the Netherhall School, Cambridge) and Caroline Duck, Year 12, for permission to use the Listening Log; p56 Syndicat d'Initiative, Vannes; p57 Librairie Arthème Fayard; p73 Juliet Davies (Goffs School, Cheshunt) for the grammar table she used in term one, Year 12, and for ideas for solo work on p79.

In some cases it has not been possible to trace copyright holders of material reproduced in this book. The publisher will be pleased to make the appropriate arrangement with any copyright holder whom it has not been possible to contact at the earliest opportunity.

First published 2001 by the Centre for Information on Language Teaching and Research (CILT), 20 Bedfordbury, London WC2N 4LB

ISBN 1 902031 60 1

2004 2003 2002 2001/10 9 8 7 6 5 4 3 2 1

A catalogue record for this book is available from the British Library

Printed in Great Britain by Copyprint (UK) Ltd

CILT Publications are available from: **Central Books**, 99 Wallis Rd, London E9 5LN. Tel: 020 8986 4854. Fax: 020 8533 5821. Book trade representation (UK and Ireland): **Broadcast Book Services**, Charter House, 27a London Road, Croydon CR0 2RE. Tel: 020 8681 8949. Fax: 020 8688 0615.

> **P** > All pages marked with this symbol are photocopiable for use with your students.

Acknowledgements

It would have been impossible to have written this book without the help and advice of teachers and of many student teachers on the PGCE Modern Languages and European Teacher Programmes at Homerton College, Cambridge. I would especially like to thank my French and Austrian students from the 1998–99 European Teacher Programme who wrote the lists of French and German expressions for oral and written presentations; Julia Whyte, a modern languages teacher from the Netherhall School in Cambridge and Caroline Duck in her Year 12 French group, for the completed Lower Sixth Listening Log; Linda Fisher, my colleague in Homerton, and other German and Austrian students for German source materials; Malcolm Hope, John Kinnear (also for providing the Spanish examples in Appendix 2), Tony Lonsdale, Anneli McLachlan and Glenis Shaw for their inspiration and ideas from several CILT conferences on teaching for A level; and Ted Neather and Emma Rees for editorial help and constructive criticism. Particular thanks must go to Ros Walker for the sections on integrating ICT into AS and A level teaching. Final thanks to my wife, Gwenneth, for putting up with the loss of weekends and evenings to enable me to write the book.

Introduction
At the beginning ...

When new students start their advanced level studies they have had a variety of modern language learning experiences. Some have gained top grades in their GCSE and are thus competent to talk, write, read and listen with comprehension when confronted with, at least, the range of topics listed in the GCSE syllabi. Some have been less successful. Athough quite confident in, say, listening and speaking, they may have problems in writing accurately. Comparatively few will have read any long texts, such as stories or even factual descriptions. Reading for fun, although encouraged by teachers, is not a common feature of many students' Modern Foreign Language (MFL) experience.

Many of the present generation, especially those with good grades in the GCSE are capable of expressing themselves using the present, perfect, imperfect and some form of the future tense in French/German/Spanish for example. Few, at present, have the necessary terminology to talk about many of the grammatical features which categorise and describe the language they are learning.

So what are the different approaches required by these students? And what should be the teacher's aims in the first few weeks of the post-16 course?

Students' needs

Post-16 advanced students will need slightly different approaches to their work especially given the detailed requirements of the Specifications (syllabi) for AS and A2 (the courses and examinations which students in Years 12 and 13 will follow and take). What is more emphasised at 16+ is:

- a greater understanding of and emphasis on **grammatical awareness, understanding and accuracy** in the productive use of language (speaking and writing);

- the ability and willingness to **read and listen to extended texts** on a range of subjects. To use available time economically and efficiently, longer texts must be the source of language and of ideas. Students will also need to have experience of reading different types of text to include at least narrative, informative, descriptive texts as well as journalese;

- the willingness and the ability of students to **work independently** and to develop the skills to learn on their own. Study skills and learning strategies must be made explicit, monitored and practised regularly. The responsibility for this must be the learners' once the teacher has shown them what to do and how to do it.

Teachers' aims

For these three aims to be met and to build on what the students can already do well, in the first few weeks of the post-16 course, teachers should try to:

Discover quickly the students' strengths and go from the known to the unknown

Many post-16 students have developed and continue to develop a range of study skills in other subjects, or they may need to see that some skills are common to all the subjects they are studying. Time spent by teachers discovering what other subjects are focusing on in these important areas can help the students (and the teachers) make the links and develop skills which help them in several curriculum areas. That is the purpose of the Key Skills initiative.

Start with what the students can do

A starter topic could be the Media, which is common to most Specifications. This may well be familiar from GCSE but will be looked at from a different angle. To inspire confidence by familiarity there could be a focus on, e.g. the Family, where the vocabulary is not completely unknown. Using film might be a novel way to explore this topic since there are several films which focus on a family and relationships within it. Other more familiar media could include articles, extracts from television, poetry, songs, paintings, etc.

Comparisons can be made to illustrate how different media treat similar topics. Text sources may dominate but other media should be included, for example:

- film extracts, recorded off-air – by students as well as by the teacher;

- texts from newspapers (e.g. the Reuters Business Briefing package for schools; it costs money but the service sifts information on any subject and sends it to the school; phone Reuters);

- *Authentik* and *Etincelle:* excellent printed and cassette material which students can take home, and read and listen to on their own, now also available on-line;

- Satellite TV (you may not have it in school but do any of the students have it at home?);

- magazines (a link school, twin town, friendly Tourist Information Office may be persuaded to send what they no longer want, especially if this is on a reciprocal basis). Ask students from exchange schools if they will send any unwanted magazines; the response is normally overwhelming and just for the cost of the postage;

- Internet, from which a variety of resources can be taken, including some of the above.

Other familiar themes which can be explored using a variety of source materials include Food and Drink, Education, Work, etc, all of which were part of previous learning experiences but can now be treated in a new way.

Let students find learning material as well as you

If students are given the responsibility for finding sources and examples of language, it can lead to some original material which can be used in class. Texts, poems, even extracts from films which they choose, given careful criteria negotiated between the teacher and the students, can be really motivating. In a project designed to encourage student choice, materials selected by one post-16 group included extracts from films (on loan from the local library), poems (found in the modern languages resources area in the school library), lyrics from songs (brought in by the Foreign Language Assistant (FLA)) and articles (printed from the Internet). Other groups had links with classes in different parts of the world (via Internet – see Chapter 6) and made francophone speakers in Montréal, la Nouvelle Calédonie and Marseille do all the work!

Tackle grammar and grammatical knowledge – revise and add

It is for the teacher to initiate a systematic, weekly programme of grammatical awareness, rule formation and practice based on an understanding of what the students need. However, it is not only the teacher who can help students; others include the FLA, adults who may be native speakers (they may not always understand the problem but can give good examples), and student-teachers who often enjoy the contact with Year 12 and Year 13 students. They recognise their problems, are willing to spend the time to explain and are effective in suggesting practical ways to improve their grammatical knowledge.

Set short and long term goals

Students need help with setting realistic targets and monitoring their progress as well as with planning their work and meeting deadlines. Many teachers have procedures in place where targets are agreed with students and monitored every week or every fortnight. This systematic and organised approach has several advantages. Students:

- take responsibility for identifying where their needs lie;
- know that someone is supporting them;
- see progress in small but realisable steps;
- log their improvement.

Find out what students know

Students' learning, in short, is best improved if teachers can find out what students know. How is this to be achieved?

Ask the students how they like to work

Students' experience of modern language learning always includes working with a partner to rehearse the spoken language. This is common practice. A look, however, at what students do in other subject areas shows a number of different forms of collaborative working, most of which support and enhance learning. Small groups in history discuss and evaluate evidence to decide questions like: *Cromwell: hero or villain?* English teachers ask pupils to work together, in and out of lessons, to analyse texts paying particular attention to language and the effects it creates for a reader. In science, often as early as in primary school, pupils are encouraged to write an account of what they did in a science lesson as a collaborative writing activity; individual pupils are encouraged to comment on and try to improve the accuracy of their collective observation, the language used when describing what has taken place and what will be the most appropriate style or format in which to present their findings. Modern languages teachers can adopt similar practices. In lessons, key ideas and key language in a text can be identified and agreed collectively. Post-16 students can be given collaborative tasks to do during their private study time. Groups, rather than individuals, can work in or out of lesson time on collaborative writing where questions of style, appropriate vocabulary, accurate use of grammatical features, an appropriate structure for specific kinds of written work can be negotiated and agreed by those participating. If this is done in a computer room and if more than one group is present, group A can spend twenty minutes on a collaborative writing task, then change seats with group B who edit and (hopefully) improve what group A has written. If both groups print out each draft the teacher can comment on the quality of the changes made, not only monitoring what each group has done but discussing the merits or otherwise of the editing.

To help all our students learn in a variety of different ways we need to take into account what skills they have learnt in other curriculum areas, often developed over a number of years. We should decide what is most efficiently done solo, in pairs and in small groups. The students, themselves, often make constructive suggestions. We should share with our learners why we choose for them to work in different ways. We must also allow them to evaluate what we propose and why they need to take more responsibility now for their own learning. More can be done to involve them in the process.

Discover what activities the students liked doing last year

With the intention of building on strengths and bridging gaps it is often helpful to identify which language activities have featured in students' pre-16 language learning experience. If some or all of the following are rated as useful or are perceived as being of little value, a short time finding out why students think as they do may provide helpful insights when planning in-school and out-of-school activity:

speaking
- [ ] with a partner
- [ ] with the FLA

reading
- [ ] in class
- [ ] at home
- [ ] for information
- [ ] for fun

listening
- [ ] to tapes
- [ ] in class
- [ ] at home
- [ ] for information
- [ ] for fun

watching
- [ ] films
- [ ] video

writing
- [ ] in class
- [ ] for homework

learning
- [ ] in class
- [ ] for homework

using computer
- [ ] in class
- [ ] for self-study

Assess the students' study skills already acquired

Having discovered what students know, the teacher's task is to refine that knowledge, add new knowledge, demonstrate progression and profile success.

Within the activities listed above a number of study skills need to be identified and assessed. Perhaps one of the most important of these is using a dictionary. While the skill and experience of using a bilingual dictionary is commonplace using a monolingual dictionary is not. This needs to be taught as do all dictionary skills, and can effectively be done collaboratively; students should be working together and, if possible, with the FLA.

Make the most of ICT

In this book, suggestions are made for the use of Information and Communications Technology (ICT). Wherever this is appropriate and helps learning it has been included and is shown by a thick vertical stripe. The main forms ICT takes are:

- **TV:** cable, Satellite and digital TV, often carrying foreign language channels, are now in widespread use. Ask students to find out what they have available at home. They may also have access to DVD films, which often carry a foreign language option;

- **text manipulation:** this can help in recreating a story from some given language, changing a dialogue into a report, inserting link words, e.g. *et, donc, mais, tandis que, si ..., cependant, qui, pour que ...* into a text, changing notes into continuous prose ... It also offers opportunities to explore different combinations of language, as well as to work from draft to finished copy;

- **CD-ROMs/WWW:** this provides information on a wide range of topics giving opportunities for students to access up-to-date texts on given topics or topics of their own choice;

- **electronic communications:** this encompasses both e-mail and videoconferencing, both of which facilitate contact with native speakers of the target language.

For these resources to be used effectively extensive consultation is needed with students for an adequate description of their learning needs. This should be timed, say, at the beginning and end of each term in Year 11 – if possible – then certainly in Years 12 and 13. Learners' needs change over time as students become more aware of their learning processes; this progression needs to be considered.

It can be assumed now with relative confidence that a student embarking upon studies at Advanced level will have had some exposure to the use of computers in their learning. The National Curriculum states that *students should be given opportunities to apply and develop their ICT capability through the use of ICT tools to support their learning in all subjects.* However, we cannot take it for granted that students will have had any experience of independent learning using computers – and yet this is just such an area where computers can be extremely valuable.

While there is, as yet, no explicit requirement to use ICT with post-16 students in their language studies, there is an implicit understanding that computers will be used as a tool in study at this level. There is also the issue of Key Skills required by students post-16 and ICT is one of these skills (www.qca.org.uk/keyskills/).

Helping students to use ICT effectively in their learning involves similar approaches as those mentioned in the introduction, but with particular reference to computers:

- **Find out how much students already know** about using computers in their studies and aim to build on those strengths. As a language teacher, it is important to use the ICT available but not to spend a lot of valuable language lesson-time teaching computing skills. In each case, the teacher must weigh up the balance between teaching an ICT skill that will allow a student to access/process language material and the amount of time spent teaching that skill.

  E.g. time spent teaching a student to use a target-language search engine will enable the student to source their own target-language materials throughout the course. This is valuable training. (See p20 for information on how to search for materials in the target language.)

- **Establish the level of access that students have to ICT.** We cannot assume that all students have access to computers, e-mail and an Internet connection. While it would be nice to make this assumption and we are aware that more and more students have access from home, it is essential not to discriminate against those students who have limited access. This may require some prior planning with the school, college and students to establish what provision exists. Make sure that students are aware of their entitlement and how they can gain access – giving out times of availability and the name of a contact for support should be sufficient.

- **Establish how students like to work with computers:** What tasks have students already tried in languages classes? What did they enjoy? What did they not enjoy? How confident will they feel in using computers in their learning?

You may like to use the checklist on the opposite page (adapting it to your institution) in order to establish your students' levels of competence in the use of computers and their level of access to appropriate hardware and software.

Checklist of computing skills for students entering advanced level study in languages

	Yes	No
WORD PROCESSING		
Can you type a piece of work in the target language with accented characters?	☐	☐
Do you know how to copy and paste between the Internet and your word processor or other applications?	☐	☐
ELECTRONIC COMMUNICATIONS		
Do you have an e-mail address?	☐	☐
Do you know how to send and receive an e-mail with attachments?	☐	☐
Do you have an e-mail partner who speaks the target language?	☐	☐
INTERNET		
Have you ever looked at a web page in the target language before now?	☐	☐
Do you know how to use a search engine to find materials in the target language?	☐	☐
CD-ROMS/SOFTWARE		
Do you ever use CD-ROMs or other software specifically designed for studying languages?	☐	☐

If yes, which ones?

>

OTHER

	Yes	No
Do you ever use computers for planning/organising your work?	☐	☐
Do you have access to a computer with Internet at home?	☐	☐
Do you feel that you are competent in using a computer?	☐	☐

(If 'No' – what extra support/training do you think you need?)

>

Name	E-mail address

checklist

1

Autonomy and confidence – learning how to learn: becoming independent

Organising and planning work

 Schools invariably have systems in place from early years to ensure that students develop good working practices. Homework diaries, monitored in school and at home, are commonplace. However, post-16 students have to extend these skills, hopefully already acquired, and develop regular work patterns. They also need to decide which work is best done at school – and when – and which best done at home, given all the other conflicting interests which they have. Although this may sound obvious, some post-16 students need to be led in a systematic and explicit way from a structured way of working suggested by the teacher to one which is decided mostly by the student. It is only like this that independence can be used efficiently. This is particularly important when progress needs to be rapid. Often a rapidly completed weekly planning framework (as shown opposite), checked regularly by a teacher, is a helpful aid towards this independence.

The thinking behind this approach, discussed openly with the student, is that the timetable of work:

- is **negotiated regularly** and is therefore realistic – using timetabled slots and non-timetabled time in school, as well as time at home (to allow for the student's social life!); if three hours' private study is considered appropriate this time initially needs planning and monitoring. If the student is trying to learn it is often better to do **a little often** than to spend long periods of time trying to commit language to memory. All tasks should be related to the targets identified and agreed;

- records **stages needed to complete** work taking account of when it has to be handed in. Explicit stages may need to be discussed initially so that the student sees exactly not only the processes required but how long each is likely to take.

Weekly planner	Language	

Name		Week beginning	

Work set		Date due in	

Personal Targets   Discussed with

1 _____   _____

2 _____   _____

Action plan   Time allocated

1 _____   _____

2 _____   _____

Discussed with   Date

Class time is only a starting point; what is worked on afterwards really counts. The approach also allows students to set and meet deadlines, thus to take responsibility for their own learning.

When this practice has become established and especially when coursework and/ or examinations are being prepared this will need to be extended and become a **term by term** planner.

Organising and planning work on computers

If students keep their records and do their work on a computer as many will, they should be encouraged to develop good 'housekeeping' skills on their computers, disks or in their own area on the school/college server. 'My computer crashed' or 'I couldn't find my file' seem to have replaced the 'my dog ate it' excuse for not handing in work. Students should be encouraged to save work regularly and systematically. They should also look at systems for backing up work. It is beyond the scope of this work to discuss the technical details of such systems but they should be discussed with an ICT co-ordinator/manager.

Students may like to look at keeping their weekly planners on computer as these can be quickly and easily updated. Some students now e-mail these planners to their tutors where this facility is available.

Keeping records and charting progress

Every teacher will have a way of monitoring a student's progress and keeping a record of what has been done. A system which allows this monitoring and assessment to be shared with the student on a weekly or fortnightly basis is an effective way of enabling precise targets to be set by teacher and student, either together or independently. Sometimes these will focus on personal organisation, sometimes on language, sometimes on extended reading, etc.

Systematic improvement

Students need working procedures which are systematic. They also need a regular programme of language input which they keep a record of and which the teacher sees. Teachers have all kinds of ways of encouraging good practice. Some are shown below.

Improving particular skills

Charts which encourage regular listening and reading are important. These can be filled in by the student (see the example opposite devised by Julia Whyte and filled in most impressively by Caroline Duck in Year 12, at the Netherhall School in Cambridge).

Logs such as this can be commented on by the teacher or by the FLA, in writing or in discussion. They are helpful guides as to how much is being done by the student, what kind of content is being encountered and what direction can be advised based on what has been achieved. It is important that if such a system is in place the teacher or FLA responds in writing (and, if possible, in discussion) to the content of what has been listened to or read. A blank version of a listening record, which can be translated into the target language, might look like the example on p14.

LOWER SIXTH LISTENING LOG

Listening skills are the hardest to develop because you cannot see the words as they are spoken. However, now that you have your own copies of AUTHENTIK and the tapes to go with them there is far more that you can do to practise these skills on your own! Remember that a substantial amount of your exam will be spent on listening....... it makes sense therefore to develop these skills.

♦ aim to do 15-20 minutes a day (IT IS FINE TO LISTEN TO PARTS OF THE RECORDING - YOU DO NOT HAVE TO DO THE WHOLE THING)
♦ choose passages from AUTHENTIK with a star rating of * to *** (see contents page of transcription)
♦ LISTEN to extract first
♦ READ the transcript (look up the words you do not understand)
♦ LISTEN again <u>without</u> the transcript
♦ LISTEN <u>with</u> the transcript
♦ FINALLY listen <u>without</u> the transcript.

Fill in the log below with the DATE and the TIME that you spent on the task and indicate which EXTRACT YOU LISTENED TO. You have had 3 copies of AUTHENTIK so far ...... you have plenty of material to choose from! This log will be checked

DATE	TIME SPENT	EXTRACT (FROM WHICH ISSUE?)
31.1.00	25 mins	A6 : Incendies *** Sep/Oct 99
1.2.00	25 mins	A7 : Part b : Starlines l'impact sur consomme *** S/O
2.2.00	20 mins	A8 a) déliquance juvénile *** sep/oct
3.2.00	10 mins	A8 b) *** - ciwis -
5.2.00	15 mins	A3 : Informations *** Nov/Dec 99
7.2.00	20 mins	A7 : France Télécom *** Nov/Dec 99
10.2.00	20 mins	A6 : Publités **** J/F 00
14.2.00	25 mins	A9 : Boeuf anglais *** J/F 00
15.2.00	10 mins	A11 : Jeux video sur Internet J/F **
6.3.00	15 mins	A12 : Météo J/F *** ½
7.3.00	15 mins	A12 : Météo J/F *** ½
8.3.00	15 mins	A13 : la coupe du Monde de rugby J/F ** (i)
9.3.00	10 mins	A14 : Musique : Simon Rattle à Berlin J/F ***
13.03.10.	Excellent Catherine. Keep this up - you won't regret it !!!	
13.3.00	15 mins	A14 . Music : Simon Rattle + a T.F. ½°
19.3.00	25 mins	B1 : Informations *** J/F -
21.3.00	15 mins	B2 : Tennis : hommes *** (*) J/F
24.3.00	25 mins	B2 : Tennis : féminin *** (1) J/F
21.3.00	25 mins	C? ; ... ***
30.3.00	20 mins.	B4 : Raissa Gorbatchev J/F ***
31.3.00	20 mins	B7 : ... *** J/F ***
2.4.00	15 mins .	B8 : Métier : interprète *** J/F ½
3.4.00	10 mins	08 ½ ***
5.4.00	10 mins	B9 : bad suite 1st interview *** J/F ∈ very good choice

NE TRICHEZ PAS! SOYEZ HONNÊTE!

Listening record for _____ (language)

Name _____

Class _____

For each entry note briefly:
- what you listened to
- date
- what it was about

If you find a particularly informative, surprising, emotive, comic, engaging

extract tell someone else about it. Say who: _____

	Source	Title	Content	Date
1				
	Comment			
2				
	Comment			
3				
	Comment			
4				
	Comment			
5				
	Comment			

The ways listening can be used to provide information and language models for students to imitate on their own for vocabulary, structures, pronunciation/ intonation, etc will be explored in detail in Chapter 3.

The purpose of such a chart may be summarised as:

- producing **evidence** of listening for the teacher and/or FLA and, most importantly, developing a **personal record** to map progress and maintain morale;
- exploring **resources**;
- recording a **range of content**;
- expressing **opinion**;
- emphasising **positive achievement**, after setting **further personal targets**.

Using other people to improve own learning and performance, including setting guidelines to clarify the teacher's role, how to access help ...

There are some students who have no hesitation in asking any teacher for help at all times of the day. Others may be more reticent either because they are shy or lack the confidence or sometimes do not know whom to approach. Initial written guidelines produced by all members of a modern languages department can specify who offers what kind of help, and when this is available in timetabled 'Surgery times'. Where such a system exists it is clear that this benefits the less and the more able alike since, if attendance is voluntary, most students will, at some stage, ask for help or just be seeking confirmation that they are working on the right lines.

It may be, in addition to normal guidance offered in class, that:

- asking for help and extending a student's language can be done at certain times with the **FLA** as well as with **other teachers in the MFL department**; contact with other members of a school staff as well as with the FLA can be more neutral than working with the teacher with whom the student is in regular contact;

- working with a **partner,** completing some tasks with someone else can be valuable and often promotes a degree of analysis and critical awareness which benefits both participants. Joint work of this kind may initially need to be developed in class so that the criteria on which judgements are based can be discussed and agreed. After such preparation partner work in listening, speaking and writing is normally very productive;

- working with **partners in the target language country** using e-mail; exchanging information in the target language, each student using his or her native language when providing information, or doing some activities together in either language is technologically straightforward. Such contacts often have a genuine appeal and can be changed as often as the students wish without offence or retribution. Contact addresses are now readily available and details are given in the bibliography.

Using other people to improve own learning and performance: making your course a community

It is becoming increasingly common for teachers to maintain a 'webpage' for a course. This can contain e-mail details for other students, facilitating contact within the group. Where an FLA is present, he or she often enjoys joining in and facilitating discussion on-line with such a group. Regular messages from the teacher can provide encouragement, motivation and reminders (!) to the students between lessons.

Building up a sense of achievement and enjoyment

In all that has been said so far the emphasis has been on self-improvement. This implies a motivated and conscientious student willing and able, on the whole, to analyse and extend his or her own learning potential. Not all of our learners are like this. Motivation itself needs to be developed. Targets are best when they are short, frequent and achievable. It is clear, too, that the more targets are set by the students themselves the greater the sense of achievement; students do however need help in setting targets which they can realistically achieve in the short term. We need to do this sensitively so that success is almost guaranteed but nonetheless does promote identifiable improvement. A system for acknowledging good performance should be in place. This may take a number of forms:

- teachers' comments in the target language on students' written work which include **acknowledgement of what is positive,** for example:
  - good range of information given;
  - clear expression of personal opinion;
  - adventurous use of language either in terms of grammatical complexity or choice of expression or use of linking words, etc, shown with a highlighter pen.
  The teachers' comments need to be a **response to the content** of the written

piece as well as to the use of language. Such comments are most motivating when they include **reference to previous targets** and an acknowledgement of those which have been achieved;

- a place to **display, anonymously, if wished, written work** not just as wall decoration but as **texts for others to read,** with opportunity for other students to comment; A5 sheets of paper under a collection of written descriptions of, for example, *The ideal job applicant,* can provoke discussion and comments by members of other classes, older or younger, if a teacher creates and makes use of such an opportunity;

- **contributions to a resource base, bulletin board, or electronic forum** where students, in written or oral form, **tell fellow students or someone else, other than the teacher, something they have researched or found interesting as a normal part of their work;** how they use the Internet, how to get the best from a specific software package, how to find out information on ..., how to write a letter in the target language requesting information from a Tourist Information Office. On a more creative level and reflecting some of the topics in the advanced syllabi, if they have been to the foreign country they can advise prospective visitors where to go for the best clothes, shoes, food, entertainment in the local town with reasons, a justification for their choice and illustration as appropriate. This also helps develop interest in the target language culture;

- an opportunity to say in the target language in detail **what they have learnt to do** in a given period of time (in October, in a term, etc); this can be kept as a personal record and also displayed from time to time. Prospective post-16 foreign language learners can, in this way, see what it is possible to achieve without a teacher having to do the publicity;

- students can create a portfolio of their own work on a website. This can be linked to the teacher's front page and can be used to display samples of work related to the students' own favourite websites. Students could have an opportunity at the end of each term to present and share the work they have done on their site – this gives them an audience for the work and a useful resource to share within the group;

- an opportunity to **work with younger children/other learners.** Some schools make very constructive use of post-16 students with younger classes to support pupils during their lessons. Channel 4's *Learning Strategies* series featured 17 and 18 year old students helping Year 7 and 8 pupils with written classwork where they explained to pupils needing help what was required in the lesson activity – where pupils could improve, which spellings needed correction, etc.

Their presence in the class was positive; the fact that they took part in the whole lesson was useful revision for them and some reassurance for the teacher that the advanced students would not make mistakes themselves (!). It also offered welcome support to the teacher and help for the younger learners who benefited from the individualised attention. Writing stories for younger pupils is also a way of integrating text and pictures, a useful way to develop reading skills (Roots in Grenfell (ed), 1995).

Having suitable access to materials and resources for developing independence in studying

The presence of self-access facilities is becoming more widespread. These facilities extend beyond what has traditionally been offered by a school library to include access to audio, video and computing resources. Many students profit greatly from using such materials. However, there can often be a mismatch between the provision of open-learning facilities and the use that students make of them. It is not enough simply to provide resources – there must be an ethos of independent learning both inside and outside the classroom. Students must be equipped with skills, as discussed in this book, and the matching resources – often backed-up with guidance and support to make the best possible use of appropriate materials.

Further information on making self-access work can be obtained through the SMILE (Strategies for Managing an Independent Learning Environment) project available at www.hull.ac.uk/langinst/smile/index.htm.

Computers are playing an increasingly important role within the area of open-access study and this is an area which will be considered in the later chapters.

key points

- Organise and schedule work **with** the students.
- Together, devise systems for improving particular skills.
- Encourage students to work with each other and external contacts.
- Increase motivation by helping students to share positive experiences.
- Establish and plan how students can best access ICT to develop independence in studying as well as sharing resources.

2

Research and study skills

Why do it?

There are two principles which underpin the necessity to develop research and study skills:

- students need to develop **ideas and language** together;
- advanced level requires more than a teacher can provide so students need to know how to work on their own.

Research skills: sourcing materials

The School Resource Centre

- Printed materials such as books (non-fiction and fiction at a range of levels, including children's/teens books used selectively), newspapers, magazines, journals.
- Multimedia materials: CD-ROMs.
- Audio materials: cassettes, videos, Satellite TV.

Students may need training in how to use the library cataloguing system to find appropriate materials and how to work effectively with some of the above resources. A library/resource centre tour should be an important part of induction into higher level study.

Local libraries may also have some of the above resources and students should familiarise themselves with what is available.

WWW

The Internet now provides the largest single resource-base available for students and for teachers. This is very good news in terms of making target-language materials more widely accessible. However, there are skills involved in obtaining these materials efficiently.

Target Language Search Engines: encourage students to search on particular topics in the target language.

French	German	Spanish
www.yahoo.fr	www.dino-online.de	www.ole.es
www.nomade.fr	www.yahoo.de	www.vindio.com
www.lokace.fr	www.hurra.de	www.yahoo.es
	www.web.de	www.biwe.es

www.google.com (select language to search in)

Developing search skills on the Internet

The Internet can provide extremely valuable and relevant material; it can also be very distracting and frustrating. Students will need to develop skills in **skimming and scanning** materials to isolate those which are most relevant to their studies. It is also important to develop skills in **searching effectively** by selecting the correct search 'string' – the word they are searching for. For example searching for information on a town, if the student types in 'Berlin' – they will receive huge amounts of information on everything relating to Berlin – the search can be narrowed down by typing:

Berlin tourist   or   Berlin history   or   Berlin government

This can be done in the form of a quiz. Give students twenty questions about target-language culture that they are unlikely to know the answer to:

- Who wrote x?
- Name eight countries where x is spoken.
- What is the currency of x?
- Who is the foreign minister in x?
- What important historical event took place in x in 1812?
- Name one tabloid and one broadsheet newspaper available in x.

- What is the weather like today in x?
- Can you tune into a radio station broadcasting in x?
- What is the main news item today in x?

Time spent in developing these skills will mean that students are better equipped to do their own research and study independently as the course goes on. You may also like to refer students to some sites which can help them to develop their search skills. Talk to other departments about how they introduce students to these skills – there may well be some overlap which could be covered with a cross-curricular approach.

Recording information and keeping notes

All that has been suggested so far implies five areas which require explicit and systematic development. These are:

- improving note-taking skills;
- keeping notes;
- keeping information;
- learning information;
- using a dictionary.

Improving note-taking skills

If notes are to serve a purpose in language learning then they need to be focused, succinct, organised and accurate. If the source can be read or listened to more than once, which is nearly always the case, the first time can be to gain an **overview,** to find meaning wherever possible; the second time can be to focus on **particular ideas or themes,** preferably decided before listening or reading; the third time can be to focus on the **language** used, including special features if this is appropriate. A fourth and final reading or listening helps **fill gaps** identified previously. If students know that they should approach the texts in this way then what they do becomes systematic. There is, however, the disadvantage that, if the same formula is rigidly applied on every occasion the activity becomes tedious. Here is where the skill of the teacher is needed to add variety which can take many forms, some of which are shown below.

Role of the teacher – encouraging an overview

The teacher can provide:

- true/false statements in the target language which summarise the content of the text;

  Advantages
  > the overall content may be expressed in different words or simpler ways from those used in the original, a skill which students need to develop;
  > the language of the true statements, written by the teacher, is an accurate summary, both linguistically and in terms of content, of what has been read or heard.

- a brief skeleton text in the target language which gives the main points, themes, aspects covered in the text which students tick if they have been understood or leave blank if they have not; after reading or listening three more times most or all aspects will be ticked;

  Advantages
  > ways of writing notes which concentrate on succinct formulation of ideas, omission of superfluous language, etc are modelled for the students to explore; these can be used as a basis for discussion about note-taking techniques afterwards;
  > what has not been ticked forms the focus of the fourth reading or listening; this shows that note-taking can become a fuller record if the source is read or heard on several occasions; it is not necessarily a one-off activity.

Role of the teacher – emphasising particular themes or ideas

The teacher can provide:

- more **detailed statements** in the target language which can be ticked if true or left blank if not true;

  Advantages
  > as above; the statements also serve to focus on certain points and confirm understanding which, in turn, builds confidence as well as reinforces language.

- **themes presented using bullet points**; students decide which are key and which are secondary in importance;

  Advantages   > the technique of using bullet points is illustrated, as is the form of language appropriate to this presentation;

                               > decisions about key elements focus attention on what can be omitted and what needs to be included during note-taking practice; this aspect is also one worth discussing **and rehearsing** in class.

- a **report** which accurately summarises some parts of the original text but summarises other parts inaccurately;

  Advantages   > again meaning remains the focus here and the activity can be done with a partner or in groups.

  Disadvantages > the report format often changes the tense of the original, which can cause problems if the linguistic complexity becomes too great, or greater than that of the original.

- **two reports:** students have to decide which one summarises the main points most accurately;

  Advantages   > as above, with a potential for useful discussion of the quality of the report and the content of the source material.

This activity can be transferred to other contexts where students compare their responses.

Learning more language

If a text is provided for either listening or reading, key language can be identified with highlighter pens using the following groupings:

- grammatical features (tenses, adverbs, adjectives …);
- useful phrases;
- text cohesion markers (*nonetheless, hereafter, so, however* …);
- semantic fields (lists of words, phrases used in particular and identified contexts);
- language functions (suasion, narration, description …).

  Advantages   > it is helpful to advanced students to analyse language according to these categories; linguistic awareness and awareness of structure is enhanced and models of language are noted for subsequent productive use in oral or written form;

> when such an awareness has been developed the way of working can be used independently of the teacher.

Gap-fill texts can be completed; to make such a task easier various possibilities are provided, with some irrelevant language.

Advantages > the focus remains on language form as well as meaning and, if the missing words are provided, the written version is more likely to be accurate, which in note-taking and language collection is essential.

Short extracts can be transcribed verbatim if the language is sufficiently useful or key.

Advantages > note-taking does sometimes require the accurate recording of key statements or quotation; practice is needed;
> the activity also helps make clear links between the written and spoken forms of the language.

Filling gaps

A final gap-fill activity identifies aspects for more focused listening or reading in order to complete previous tasks or, more generally, to reinforce meaning and linguistic awareness; it is helping to *construct that internal system that is necessary to a fully generative competence in a language* (Grenfell, 1995: 4).

The purpose of the examples shown above is twofold; the first is to make note-taking a systematic activity either in class or at home, the second is to develop in students an ability which will depend less and less on the teacher and, in time and with practice, lead to greater student independence and autonomy.

Keeping notes

Students develop their own systems for keeping notes. Some do this methodically and some do not. All students benefit from some initial guidance even if later, as we would hope, they devise their own ways of working. They should also be reminded to apply advice given in other subjects. This section considers:

- what sort of notes to take and keep;
- how to organise them;
- how to use notes.

What sort of notes to take and keep

In the discussion on improving note-taking skills the focus was on the student working from audio or written source material and taking notes.

There are, in addition to these quite specific records of what has been read or listened to, more general notes which can be added to as a term progresses. These are essentially on-going, made by the student and/or provided by the teacher which record:

ideas and the language in which these can be expressed
> where ideas and language are collected, normally during work on a topic or theme, and a record kept of new and related language as it is encountered. In addition to written notes students often find very useful an audio cassette on which they keep recordings of published materials (the school must ensure it has a site licence), or recordings made by themselves or the FLA. These can be topic-based or more general. Personal cassettes have the advantage of providing a record of audio content already encountered as well as rehearsing appropriate intonation and pronunciation;

chunks of language
> which the person taking the notes considers can be re-used verbatim; these normally consist of useful phrases, both spoken and written, which need not be restricted to any particular context, theme or topic;

ways of structuring
> in written or oral forms, facts, information, personal opinion; much time should be spent in class on how to present information and how to express opinions persuasively, and on identifying and selecting key phrases from source material. These linguistic forms need to be learnt and re-used frequently so on-going records are essential;

how to engage an audience or reader
> this might include the use of time markers, how to introduce and conclude a written or oral presentation, make openings, argue a case;

grammatical features

these will be discussed in detail in Chapter 5; however, they are mentioned here because keeping accurate grammar notes is essential.

How to organise notes: where and how to keep information

Most students find helpful a system which uses separated sections in a **card index box** (or a loose-leaf file) categorised as:

Content and language
Organised thematically (see A level Specifications) but often requiring sub-headings
Media • Advertising • The Arts • Daily Life • Food and Drink • Sport and Pastimes • Travel, transport and holidays • Human interest news items
These are OCR AS Modules; reading and listening topics

Grammar
• rules in own language
– shown in context
– identified by use of overliner/colour
– referenced to preferred grammar book
– what I never get right (but showing correct usage/mistakes corrected)

Organised for general use
• own notes organised in skill areas:
– oral phrases useful in presentations
– linking words for writing, etc
• information sheets
• printouts from media or other sources

ICT

Making notes on a word processor can help with clear presentation. Using different fonts, colours and text boxes can help to improve understanding and assist memory.

What to do with notes and how and when to make use of them: learning information

It is useful to discuss with students memorisation techniques and learning by heart. There may be ways which work better than others! If, for example, they are exploring how to memorise phrases, quotations, short texts, etc they can consider and try out different methods, and, in class, discuss those which seem to work effectively. To start groups off they can experiment with:

■ read, cover, write out and check;

■ memorise and test yourself with a friend (good for oral memorisation but not so reliable for accurate spelling);

■ write or print the text; cut into sections; jumble up and reorganise to reconstruct the original text (can be done as a cut and paste activity with a word processing package);

■ make own gap-fill exercise, starting with the original text and deleting words and phrases, or even grammatical categories (can be done as a game with a partner, and made competitive by trying to complete in the shortest time).

Imaginative students can probably invent or describe their own learning and memorisation techniques. Here is a short text which explores this theme:

Comment apprendre une langue. Quelques problèmes et quelques trucs pour les surmonter. Avec un(e) partenaire décidez les moyens les plus efficaces.

Problème 1

Mais il faut mémoriser beaucoup de mots ...

▶

Conseil:
* Lisez. Mémorisez. Cachez. Écrivez. Vérifiez.
* Coupez un texte en morceaux. Mettez les morceaux ensemble.
* Choisissez des mots ou des phrases qui sont importants pour vous. Apprenez-les.
* Racontez-vous ce qui se passe dans l'histoire.
* (Avec un ami/une amie) apprenez un texte par cœur.
* Mettez le vocabulaire dans un dialogue imaginaire.
* Inventez une histoire qui contient tout le vocabulaire que vous voulez apprendre.
* Associez les mots avec des images.
* Employez le traitement de texte.

Problème 2

Il me faut des heures et des heures pour progresser. C'est décourageant.

▶

Conseil: un quart d'heure ou vingt minutes par jour sont plus efficaces que deux heures une fois par semaine. Vous pourrez voir vos progrès plus rapidement. Peut-être que vous vous surprendrez!

Using a dictionary

A final study skill which needs both practice and discussion is using a dictionary. This will normally be building on skills already acquired, especially using a bilingual dictionary. However, the effective use of monolingual dictionaries may be new so needs careful guidance, which, when given, can be discussed in class by students working collaboratively on common problems. It is very important that teachers orchestrate such discussions initially so that effective and efficient habits are established as early as possible.

Ways of helping students to develop the necessary skills include:

■ providing texts where words are highlighted. Working in pairs, students look up words firstly in a bilingual dictionary, then in a monolingual dictionary and write down their definitions. As Tony Lonsdale (in Shaw (ed) 2000) advises, *some items will be found as they appear in the text; others will need 'converting'*. Subsequent discussion can compare what the students find in both kinds of dictionary and how the one can help the other;

■ setting dictionary-based tasks based on texts selected for their interesting content; these can be done solo or with a partner but should have a class time slot for discussion by the teacher.

Electronic dictionaries can be used very efficiently. Many will give a word used in context that can be 'clicked' and heard. It is also possible to sort and search words – for example, you would be able to list all the separable verbs in German following *an-* or look at conjugations of certain verbs in French in the subjunctive. If students are comfortable with computers, CD-ROM dictionaries can prove to be very useful.

key points

- Train students to use all resources at their disposal – print, audio, multimedia.
- Emphasise the value of the Internet if used selectively.
- Use a variety of exercises to develop note-taking skills.
- Give students basic advice on organising notes, then let them devise their own systems.
- Practise using monolingual and bilingual dictionaries solo and in collaboration with others.

3

The receptive skills of listening and reading – working with and around texts

Principles

The principles on which developing receptive skills is based are:

- the more learners interact with texts the more learning takes place; again developing language and ideas together;

- the **initial emphasis** in listening and reading is on **understanding,** not necessarily on providing detailed information;

- learners need a variety of text types and a range of topics;

- texts (oral or written) should:
  - cover a range of functions
  - be analysed with reference to their *coherence* which needs to be practised and learned
  - serve as models for speaking and writing, where possible;

- students should be encouraged to reflect on and to discuss their own learning at all stages.

A suggested **approach for students and teachers** might be divided into six steps as set out below. The approach can also be used by students working on their own. They will need to have the logic of such a model made clear, so that the presentation of the six-step model is followed by a discussion of the characteristics of reading and listening.

Six steps

Before seeing the text

1   **Brainstorm** – from photographs, headlines, title, format …

2   **Predict and list/categorise language** – what might the text be about, what language might be included (tenses, nouns …)?

With the source visible/audible

3   **Identify what you have understood** – read and listen for gist: what did you read/hear that was on your list of predictions; what information did you understand?

4   **Add to lists and categories** – what words did you read/hear that you knew but did not predict?

5   **Practise and expand** – read/listen again; can you add anything else to your list? What else did you understand? How did you guess the meaning of unfamiliar words: did you use cognates, say words aloud? If listening, did you try writing the word down? How will you go about finding out what the remaining unknown words mean?

Away from source

Perform – use the language you have read/heard to write your own version/talk about a similar topic

The justification for these six stages could be discussed in the following ways:

Brainstorming

This raises awareness of the kind of text and the kind of topic that is under discussion. When listening the first step is to decide what kind of spoken text it is – description, debate, exposition, read-aloud text … With written texts, there are photos, format, layout, headlines to help.

Certain texts are likely to contain certain types of language; newspapers do not use the same language as advertisements. Travel advertisements use a different range of vocabulary from ones designed to promote food products. A text on the dangers of smoking may include words like *tobacco, cigarette, cigar, drug, addiction, tar, health, lung cancer, breathing,* etc. See what suggestions the students make.

Prediction

Much listening and reading is facilitated by an awareness of what might be. If learners can learn to use their knowledge of the world to try to predict what is likely then they activate strategies which make the task less daunting. To use the example quoted above on the dangers of smoking, students can see how many of these words – and any others they can think of – they know already in the target language. It is advisable, however, to warn students of the dangers of taking too much for granted without considering the accompanying detail. Misinterpretation is all too easy!

Identify what you have understood

This step is designed to confirm predictions so that learners can see if the strategy works. If it does not work they can perhaps discuss why. If it is successful they are likely to try it again. It should be emphasised to students that to have understood only part is quite sufficient on the first listening or reading. If they are working from a written or an oral text they can spend time on and discuss what in the text has enabled them to derive meaning; the reading and listening strategies involved should be made explicit but are most convincing if the students discover at least some of them for themselves (see the Step on *practising and expanding* below). It is important for students to discover that the initial skill is based on gist understanding and the follow-up normally moves to understanding detail.

Add to lists and categories

Some of the language from the source material will be known but may not have been predicted. It is helpful to list what **is** known so that a positive approach is maintained and the emphasis is not just on the unknown. Such a strategy shows students that they can decipher meaning in most situations without knowing **all** the words. Underlining all the unknown words in a written text is not a helpful procedure because it both emphasises the negative and fails to provide any strategies to achieve meaning.

Practise and expand

Re-reading and listening again are essential; often it is only on a third listening or a third reading that meaning becomes clear. Strategies for finding the meaning of unknown words merit discussion, exemplification and comparison within the group; using a dictionary is not the only answer. Students can try:

- asking someone else (best done in the target language);
- discussing a guess with others in the group;
- looking at what part of speech the unknown word is;
- looking for cognates;
- reading beyond the unknown word;
- deciding that not to know the word perhaps does not make a difference, but that some words or phrases are key so need to be looked up.

If listening is the skill being practised – and listening has particular problems – students can try:

- taking note of the way in which words are said;
- paying attention to the intonation and stress which the speaker uses.

In the same way that reading is helped by headlines, photographs, etc to build up the context from as many clues as possible, the student, when listening, can do a little of this by taking into account:

- **who** is speaking;
- **when** and **where** the talk is taking place;
- **what** is being talked about;
- **how** it is being said.

Students also benefit from an awareness of pause markers and fillers, the *alors, euh … , ben, moi, je … , attends … , bof … , je sais pas, euh …* used frequently in speech in French. They should be aware that hesitation, repetition, partly completed sentences, rephrasing are common features of speech in any language. These should not impede comprehension, and are less likely to do so when students are aware how normal they are. Such an awareness can be turned into a deliberately taught aspect of modern language lessons if students are encouraged to use fillers and pause markers in their own spoken language. By using these and other features they will soon discover that they can maintain contact with their listener – since a silence is very off-putting – and create time to think out an answer or a response to a question or a remark. In other words we are encouraging them to do in the foreign language what they would do naturally and without thinking in their mother tongue. This helps their listening and their spoken language and is both effective and efficient, a theme discussed further elsewhere (see Jones in Littlewood, 1989).

As with reading skills the effectiveness of fillers can be explored in class and further strategies developed.

Perform

Having gone through these steps as a way of arriving at meaning and to add to what is already known, especially if this is a collaborative enterprise, the language of the text now needs to be used and put into operation in order to establish it as part of the students' repertoire. Writing summaries, adaptations, propaganda leaflets, advice based on what was read, or integrating the spoken language into drama and little scenarios acted out (especially good for exaggerated use of fillers), oral presentations, reports, jingles, advertisements may be worth considering. The student group should be involved not only as listeners or readers but as judges; they can evaluate how well fellow students re-use language learnt or encountered and in so doing learn to become more self critical. They must see that re-using language is an aid to learning and should be acknowledged and rewarded. Teachers can assess, too, if learning targets have been met and commend those who perform well.

In working with and around texts – aim one: to extend general knowledge and language together

Here students are encouraged to:

■ collect ideas, collect language;
■ develop a cultural dimension;
■ extend the language collected;
■ develop a grammatical awareness;
■ extend grammar and structures;
■ look at ways texts are constructed as models to be re-used.

In working with and around texts – aim two: to develop and extend reading and listening skills

Research has shown that if **reading and listening** strategies are made explicit both for and by the students and if they are developed systematically then language learning is likely to improve. *If successful learners have a wider repertoire of strategies than their less successful peers, then it seems sensible to intervene and offer them the opportunity to acquire these tools. It could be argued that making explicit to students how to go about the learning process might not only serve to increase such learners' range of strategies, it might also improve their motivation* (Grenfell and Harris, 1999: 73). However, as they also point out, *it is unrealistic to assume that simply telling students about possible fruitful strategies will ensure that these pass into their repertoire and can be drawn on automatically. Explicit reminders to use the reading strategies will be necessary alongside a number of tasks and materials likely to promote them* (ibid p77).

Reading and listening for gist

When developing and extending reading and listening skills students need to explore the differences between reading/listening for gist and reading/listening for detail. They need to realise that the purpose for reading determines the approach and the strategy to adopt. When gist understanding is involved they should be given texts for skimming and then asked what they did. Hopefully discussion will bring out the following strategies, that when reading or listening for gist they:

- did not stop every time they came across a new, unknown word;
- did not worry if they did not understand every word;
- did focus on what they had understood so they were instinctively using some appropriate strategies.

The reading or listening sources could here be magazine or newspaper articles, radio stations abroad, books to read for fun, and the task would involve listening to see which radio programme was worth tuning in to, or which newspaper article might be worth reading, or which book to choose.

Reading or listening for detail

For this activity the skill is, of course, that of scanning for particular information. Here they may need to explore what they can do to overcome difficulties. They can try when **listening:**

- writing down an unknown word;
- deciding where one word ends and another begins;
- listening for words that sound like English (very few exist in French – they may **look alike** but they do **not sound alike** – more exist in German);
- using the rest of the utterance and its structure to make a guess, thus using the familiar to help resolve the unfamiliar;
- using intonation to guess a language function, such as a question, statement, etc;
- using common sense;

and they can try when **reading:**

- saying an unknown word aloud;
- spotting look-alike words or cognates;
- using the context as in listening to help make informed guesses;
- using grammatical understanding to help;
- using punctuation;
- using common sense.

Since the emphasis here is on detail then it is this close analysis of text which can focus on acquiring new language, phrases and structures and building up a student's language resources. How this relates to developing grammatical competence will be discussed in Chapter 5.

A range of text types

Together with making explicit reading and listening skills students should have experience of different types of text and be familiar with the different conventions which are typical of each genre. It is helpful, therefore, if we ensure that students encounter a range of materials which for reading includes:

- conversational
- descriptive
- narrative
- informative
- persuasive
- journalese
- letter (business, personal)
- fax
- e-mail

and for listening:

- phone calls
- announcements
- advertisements
- news (TV, radio)
- songs.

In order to develop reading skills students need experience of reading short and longer texts as well as reading for fun. Just as reading skills are improved by several readings so listening is helped if students listen as many times as they want. In practice this means they should have their own cassettes on which favourite recordings are kept. If given a choice from all the recordings they listen to in a year they often make some original compilations.

An approach to listening and reading which helps teachers help learners

When working with spoken and written texts, teachers may like to think of ways of starting from less demanding sources and gradually build up the level of difficulty.

In the first weeks the following strategies seem to be useful. They are based on the six steps referred to above but are made relevant to students starting out on their advanced course.

Pre-reading/listening tasks for the teacher to orchestrate

Students predict from a:	headline	photograph
	advertisement	still from a film/video
	painting	poster

and brainstorm words and phrases – a strategy worth developing as early as possible since it starts from what students know, and collectively they often produce encouraging amounts of language. It is useful if teachers can prompt different grammatical categories (verbs in the infinitive, adjectives, adverbs) since students often limit themselves to lists of nouns.

The teacher teaches key phrases/vocabulary which will appear either verbatim or in similar form in the text. This language can be given out as lists and copied or ticked by the students when read or heard. Such a strategy starts the students' **collection of useful or key phrases and is an accurate record.** Can you add more activities for the pre-reading/listening stage?

During the reading/listening

Students read sentences written **by the teacher** about the general theme(s) treated in the original text. Students listen to/read the original and spot any differences or inaccuracies in the information conveyed. This is done to **encourage and refine reading or listening for gist understanding.**

Gap-fill: students listen to/read the original and fill gaps either with possibilities listed by the teacher or from memory (e.g. from a few lines of text). This helps **contextualise words or phrases** considered to be particularly useful by the teacher within the given topic or theme.

Students listen to/read the original and collect all the vocabulary to do with ... or phrases which express opinions, etc. This is to increase the language collection but this time organised into semantic categories as an aid to **memorisation.**

Students listen and transcribe some key sentences; with listening texts this helps to make a **speaking-to-writing link.**

Students listen to/read the original and say whether a number of related statements are true or false; this is another activity where the emphasis is on **developing meaning.**

Students listen to/read the original and find words which have been defined by the teacher **or** written as synonyms **or** written as antonyms – tasks usually done most efficiently by the FLA.

Students dictate a short extract; this helps also to enhance **speaking-to-writing links.**

Students listen to/read the original and find different grammatical features, e.g. all the verbs in the pluperfect tense, all the adjectives related to personal characteristics, etc, which then require **explanation** and **recontextualisation.**

Students translate small sections from English back into the French/German/ Spanish ... original and vice versa; this concentrates on the precise wording of the source material and is easily checked by the student if the source is written. If the source is spoken the emphasis can be on re-creating the intonation, phrasing, stress of the original text. Pairs of students can do this together and judge each other's performance.

After listening and reading: some suggestions for follow-up, performance activities

Students can be asked to:

- devise **questions** to write/say to the author;
- write a **summary/notes** of key ideas to give to someone else;
- produce their **own text** for an advertisement, jingle … ;
- write key phrases into sentences as part of a **report,** etc;
- report the main ideas in four (?) sentences which include a number of key phrases/vocabulary in the form of a **publicity poster;**
- have a **debate** for and against;
- list **'expressions I like'.**

Over to you!

What to read and listen to

Since language is acquired both consciously and subconsciously when reading and listening it is an efficient activity for students in terms of their learning. We will look at reading here in some detail, although what is claimed for or said about reading mostly also applies to listening.

It may be that the separation of reading into what is read for **content,** a form of **intensive reading,** and what is read for **pleasure,** or **extensive reading,** is helpful since reading strategies will differ for each. This is not to say that intensive reading should not have interesting and motivating content – because it should – but that the two forms of reading have different purposes shaped by the required outcome.

Reading for content

When reading for **content** students should have as their objectives to:

- enhance their own ideas;
- see how different writers treat particular topics and content and how their stylistic approach varies;

- develop appropriate language for their own writing or oral presentations;
- discover how text is more than a series of sentences.

Reading texts can be chosen to exemplify a range of language functions such as informing, reporting, narrating, instructing, describing. If students use reading sources such as these they can be encouraged to discover not only how these and other language functions are realised but that, if they base their own writing on language features found in a variety of models, they can operate flexibly and with conviction.

Efforts should be made not to overwhelm students with a number of texts analysed with a somewhat formulaic approach; if this happens all language seems equally vital for them to learn. Instead they should be encouraged to find and record, and subsequently use:

- a **core** of appropriate language phrases, structures and strategies which will serve in most contexts;
- **extension** language and activities which may allow them as speakers or writers to be more creative and individual.

An example

An illustration in French might look like the example on pp40-41, where the **core** activities are exemplified in activities i–iii and **extension** in activities ɪv–v. The **source materials** – and starting point – used for planning this sequence were the original texts (version B) written by three real French students, Jérémy, Natasha and Frédéric. Planning, therefore, **starts with the texts** (version B) **as a potential end product or outcome** and works back from them and by analysis to language tasks based on version A which is the simplified text without the *phrases variées* added. The student therefore progresses by steps from the simple, to the more complex, to the final outcome.

Écrire une description? Suivez le guide!

 En groupes de trois/quatre écrivez tous les adjectifs qui décrivent une région, une ville ou un village, et les habitants. Après quelques minutes chaque groupe doit écrire sa liste au tableau.

Comparez vos listes avec la nôtre. Quelles sont les différences?

ville/village	animé, animée
agréable	cher, chère
pittoresque	impressionnant, impressionnante
beau (bel), belle	grand, grande
industriel, industrielle	petit, petite
pollué, polluée	nouveau (nouvel), nouvelle
retiré, retirée	les gens, les habitants
génial, géniale	sympas
tranquille	chaleureux, chaleureuses
moderne	aimables
vieux (vieil), vieille	

 Toujours en groupes de trois/quatre écrivez des phrases très simples.

exemples:	il y a des quartiers
c'est une ville	il y a une poste
c'est un village	il y a des cafés
il y a beaucoup de magasins	il y a des touristes
il y a des magasins	c'est pollué
il y a des maisons	c'est génial
il y a la cathédrale et l'université	

 Maintenant mettez les adjectifs dans les phrases. Évitez la répétition, si possible.

exemples:	il y a une **vieille** cathédrale et une
c'est une **grande** ville	université **moderne**
c'est un **petit** village	il y a un quartier **industriel**
il y a beaucoup de magasins **vides**	il y a des quartiers **animés**
il y a de **belles** maisons	il y a des cafés **agréables**

iv Apprenez des phrases variées pour commencer vos phrases.

Ma ville est …	On voit de plus en plus de …
Là où j'habite, c'est …	Je dirais que …
Au centre-ville	A chaque instant …
Aux alentours	Il y a un côté …
En banlieue	Pour les gens qui …
En pleine campagne	On peut faire …
A la campagne	On voit …
De plus en plus on voit …	Mais …
Nous avons …	Cependant …
Il faut dire que …	Quand même …
On découvre …	

 v Commencez, si possible, chaque phrase d'une façon différente.

exemple:
Là où j'habite c'est une grande ville. On découvre de belles maisons. A chaque instant on voit des quartiers animés et des cafés agréables. Mais il y a un côté industriel. De plus en plus on voit des magasins vides et c'est pollué. Cependant pour les gens qui y habitent on ne s'y ennuie jamais. Quand même ma ville est géniale!

Et vous voilà!

Comparez maintenant les descriptions faites par Jérémy, Natasha et Frédéric dans l'Activité A (page suivante). Ils ont ajouté des phrases tirées de la quatrième liste ci-dessus. Trouvez-les et écrivez-les!

Jérémy

VERSION A

C'est une ville agréable. On peut y pratiquer des sports, il y a beaucoup de magasins … On ne s'y ennuie jamais. On découvre de très belles maisons et des quartiers pittoresques. Nous avons la cathédrale et l'université. Il y a un côté industriel qui n'est pas aussi pittoresque. C'est assez pollué. Il fournit des jobs quand même. Et pour les gens qui doivent faire la navette, il y a un très bon réseau entre la Normandie et Paris.

VERSION B

Je dirais que c'est une ville agréable. On peut y pratiquer des sports, il y a beaucoup de magasins … On ne s'y ennuie jamais. À chaque instant on découvre de très belles maisons et des quartiers pittoresques. Nous avons la cathédrale et l'université. Il y a un côté industriel qui n'est pas aussi pittoresque. Il faut dire que c'est assez pollué. Il fournit des jobs quand même. Et pour les gens qui doivent faire la navette, il y a un très bon réseau entre la Normandie et Paris.

Natasha

VERSION A

Là où j'habite, c'est un coin retiré en banlieue, loin des grandes surfaces. Il n'y a que les petits magasins, il n'y a qu'une poste, qu'un café … mais c'est génial, un paysage tranquille. Les gens sont sympas et chaleureux. Moi, j'aide mes parents dans leur travail. Quand j'ai des heures libres je me sens quelquefois isolée – mes copains au collège me manquent! On voit des touristes, surtout des Anglais. Ça me plaît. Je sais parler anglais – c'est-à-dire j'apprends l'anglais au collège – donc je peux communiquer avec eux.

VERSION B

Là où j'habite, c'est un coin retiré en banlieue, loin des grandes surfaces. Il n'y a que les petits magasins, il n'y a qu'une poste, qu'un café … mais c'est génial, un paysage tranquille. Les gens sont sympas et chaleureux. Moi, j'aide mes parents dans leur travail mais quand j'ai des heures libres je me sens quelquefois isolée – mes copains au collège me manquent! De plus en plus on voit des touristes, surtout des Anglais. Ça me plaît. Je sais parler anglais – c'est-à-dire j'apprends l'anglais au collège – donc je peux communiquer avec eux.

Frédéric

VERSION A

Ma ville est très moderne, très animée, avec beaucoup de centres commerciaux. La plupart des gens travaillent sur place, mais il y en a qui font la navette à Paris. Nous avons de grands magasins très impressionnants. Il y a des rues piétonnes. On peut bien s'amuser et faire du lèche-vitrines. La vie est chère chez nous et nous avons ressenti les effets du chômage. On voit de plus en plus de magasins vides.

VERSION B

Ma ville est très moderne, très animée, avec beaucoup de centres commerciaux. La plupart des gens travaillent sur place, mais il y en a qui font la navette à Paris. Nous avons de grands magasins très impressionnants. Il y a des rues piétonnes et on peut bien s'amuser et faire du lèche-vitrines. Il faut dire quand même que la vie est chère chez nous et nous avons ressenti les effets du chômage. On voit de plus en plus de magasins vides.

P

Reading and listening for pleasure

An initial contact with short, light-hearted and uncomplicated texts, especially if these are authentic, is often confidence-building. Students do, however, need to progress to longer books or audio texts and more challenging ideas. Systematic reading and listening is best encouraged when students have lists of what is available, maybe graded, and certainly organised thematically. Some students like guidance as to what each is about, to help them choose and decide where to start. If reading or listening for pleasure is categorised as 'an activity just to enjoy for its own sake' then, it may be argued, it should contain no activities, no tasks, no explicit analysis, no pedagogic point or predetermined outcome. This kind of activity needs books, tapes, videos to be available rather than required or compulsory; reading or listening material can be returned half-finished or parts may be skipped if they are not of interest. There should be a variety of subject matter and of styles to suit different tastes. Lively and eye-catching presentation is important for reading so that there is a willingness to engage with the text. Listening is often more appealing if it is complemented with visual representation such as photographs, cartoons or other images. The written text of an audio presentation can aid comprehension; film extracts, if accompanied by a film script, can have both a strong visual and auditory impact especially if the film is viewed first and the script read afterwards.

A teacher's ability to have on offer an attractive range of reading or listening sources may be enhanced by discovering which kinds – fact, narrative, opinion, description, instructions, etc – are preferred and how students respond to what is on offer. Students can, after a month or two, be asked to list their top ten selection based on a short appreciation of each item read or listened to, and present it to the group.

Examples of different types of reading text might include:

- poems
- puzzles
- quizzes
- questionnaires and surveys
- magazine articles
- extracts from books
- short stories.

Examples of different types of listening might include:

- guides to entertainment
- instructions for making something

- narrative
- poems read aloud
- short fictional stories, including horror, suspense
- TV programme excerpts
- puzzles.

Collecting, storing and indexing resources: guidelines for students

What to collect

In Chapter 2 there were suggestions for keeping and organising personal notes. This section focuses on **resources** – articles, photocopies, cassettes, photos, as well as examples of useful language, etc.

If reading or listening for **content** is the objective students should be encouraged to choose their own texts and resources from a variety on offer according to their interests, their need for specific language or ideas, or as material, some of which they can learn by heart.

An easy index system: keeping a record of printed and audio resources and related language

Students will also need guidance on how to help themselves.

Record-keeping and the use of a loose-leaf A4 folder with **index tabs** and pockets for audio cassettes and printed materials: using a system like this helps keep the resources and the student's ideas and language collection together. Top sheets, under each of the index tabs, such as the one shown, also provide useful reference guides for revision, or act as the basis for discussion in class or with the FLA. Opposite is a suggested format.

These resources should include a range which include:

- facts
- ideas
- opinions.

TOPIC AREA:	**SKILL:** Reading
SOURCE:	

Key ideas:

already explored

to be developed

Useful language and phrases I like:

What to work on:

revision guide

Receptive skills

The approaches already discussed in this chapter can be enhanced or developed through the use of computers.

Reading

Probably the most significant of these ways is in the amount of authentic reading material available on-line through the Internet. Students can access target-language materials on any topic that takes their interest or that is relevant to their studies (see notes in Chapter 2 on searching for materials). Let us look at some ways in which these materials can be exploited:

Resources for topic work: the Internet can be a valuable source of resources for Advanced level topic work. The following website was developed by PGCE students at Bristol University: www.bris.ac.uk/Depts/Education/ml/alevel.htm.

This contains resources for French, German, Spanish and Italian.

Each A level topic area is linked through with a brief summary and evaluation.

Example from the French section

Le cinéma

Chabrol's films (www.ecran-noir.com/real/france/chabrol.htm)

On-line • Off-line • Print-out •

Suitable for:
Teachers • Students •

Summary of content:
A chronological list of Chabrol's films and a potted biography of the director. There are also links to sites about his two most recent films: *Au coeur du mensonge* and *Rien ne va plus.*

Activities:
Useful for reading practice, in particular for skimming and scanning. For example the teacher could ask *'Quel film a-t-il réalisé en 1977?'* The site is useful to teachers because it contains helpful background information.

Many teachers and students are now building up their own banks of Internet links and resources in line with the new AS/A2 exams. Keeping in touch with other teachers through a discussion list such as Lingu@NET-forum (see Bibliography) can help you to keep up-to-date with the resources available. Your exam board may also run a website for students.

Classroom ideas

Try dividing your topic into sections and asking pairs or groups in the class to focus on different aspects of it, producing oral presentations and handouts for the rest of the group, e.g. if you are looking at Politics in the country, one group may look at the right-wing, another group looks at the left-wing, another group concentrates on other main-stream parties and one group looks at extreme parties. Again, students can develop their own search skills to source materials on these topic areas, but they may initially need some support in doing this.

Students can e-mail each other texts that they find on particular topics, helping each other to build up a bank of resources.

Students can work with a file in *Fun with Texts* and reading comprehension questions from the teacher. Using these questions, they have to deduce the content of the text in *Fun with Texts* and build the text back up in order to answer the questions.

Listening

At present, listening using computers is slightly restricted by sound quality and the size of many sound files. Real Audio is the most efficient mode of transmission over the Internet. Sound can also be stored on the hard disk of the computer and makes accessing sound files very easy.

Provide *Fun with Texts* files linked to a listening file – either on cassette or loaded into the computer. Students can listen to the file and work on building up the text simultaneously. This is very nice to do from materials such as *Authentik* which supplies texts and listening materials together.

Students can access **Internet radio and news broadcasts** over the Internet. Simply listening to these will help them to gain much more of a feel for the language. Listening repeatedly and attempting to transcribe the text can help students to hone their listening skills in the way that a more traditional *dictation* would do.

- http://ds.dial.pipex.com/town/place/abn39/ra.htm – Mike's Radio World – a large collection of links to many radio stations where students can listen live. This requires a Real Audio Player (free download from www.ra.com).

- www.bbc.co.uk/worldservice/index.shtml – BBC World service link to news in French and Spanish – audio and written.

key points

- Move from reading and listening for gist to reading and listening for detail.
- Adopt a *six-step* approach to reading and listening.
- Use a range of text types.
- Build up the level of difficulty with a variety of tasks.
- Adopt a systematic approach pre/during/post listening and reading.
- Encourage students to build up their own collection of language resources.
- Mine the Internet for authentic reading and listening material.

Productive skills: speaking and writing

Principles

- Spoken or written expression/communication should have a known **audience** (listener or reader) and a clear **purpose.**

- That which is spoken or written is a context for developing grammatical accuracy.

- Students need to build up their confidence particularly in these two skill areas by:
  - working with others;
  - going from the simple to the complex;
  - learning from their performance.

Aim: to develop speaking skills

Most students when they start their advanced studies are proficient at describing themselves. They will, in most cases, have a relatively secure knowledge of how to say and describe:

- where they live;
- daily routine;
- daily diet;
- school and leisure activities;
- what they do during holiday periods.

If we take as a general principle that we:

- start gradually working from the familiar;
- relate known language to the other culture;

then it should be possible to develop an oral presentation on a personality from the target country.

An example of this may be a **presentation of a character in a film.**

Step 1: working from known and familiar language

- Presentation of self.
- Supply the information by completing the sentences below.

Commencez la présentation avec ces phrases. Complétez-les!

Je m'appelle …
J'ai … ans
J'habite à …
Dans ma famille il y a …
Tous les jours   je me lève à …
               je prends mon petit déjeuner …
               je vais à l'école en voiture …
Le soir   je mange …
        je regarde la télé
        je me couche à …
Le weekend je …
En été, pendant les grandes vacances, je …

See Appendix pp84 and 88
for German and Spanish
versions
of Steps 1 and 2

Step 2: extending known and familiar language

- Presentation of self.

Décrivez votre personnalité

 Écrivez et complétez la phrase 'Je ne suis pas … mais je suis …' en ajoutant deux adjectifs choisis dans la liste qui suit:

nerveux, nerveuse	impatient, impatiente	travailleur, travailleuse
intelligent, intelligente	sympathique	gentil, gentille
sociable	dynamique	sportif, sportive
humoriste	amusant, amusante	difficile
organisé, organisée	compréhensif, compréhensive	fainéant, fainéante
communicatif, communicative	timide	franc, franche

2 Maintenant utilisez ces mots, si possible, et rajoutez la phrase complète dans votre description personnelle.
Exemple: Je ne suis pas sympathique mais je suis assez travailleuse

pas très
quelquefois un peu
bien
assez très

3 Continuez la description; mettez la phrase à l'endroit qui convient:

parce que je suis ... (timide, organisée – à vous de choisir le mot convenable).

In other words, the beginning of this character portrait starts with known phrases and adds more detail into an existing framework by asking students to:

- find appropriate adjectives from a list of attributes;
- qualify these adjectives;
- add a phrase or phrases to the initial framework.

Step 3: extending known and familiar language

- Presentation of self.

The third step sets out to extend the language by adding expressions like:

> *Je pense que je suis ...*
> *Je voudrais être ...*
> *Si j'étais plus ... je serais moins ...;*

extend the grammatical complexity
(e.g. tense: I would like to be ...).

Diagrammatically this could be shown as:

Presentation of self

I am ... > *can be developed by* > I think I am ...
I believe I am ...

present

> use of conditional
> use of subjunctive
> use of future

I wish I were ...
I am ... but I would prefer to be ...
I am ... but I could be ...
I am ... but in the future/with more determination
I will be ...

Step 4: extending known and familiar language

- Presentation of someone else.

Now that the language has been activated extension can be both lexical and/or grammatical. In this example we have chosen a grammatical development by re-using the language practised so far to talk about someone else. For this to have any kind of communicative content it should have an **audience** and a **purpose.**

Within the A level Specifications there are frequently films, or extracts from a film, which illustrate relationships. The teacher or the students can choose an extract showing different characters and ask the class to write one or more portraits using vocabulary and structures already rehearsed. At the simplest grammatical level this involves changing first person (*je*) verb forms to the third person (*il/elle*). Of course all the details from the initial presentation of self will not be applicable; much can, however, be imagined if these are not immediately obvious. Other members of the film family, either imagined or real, can be portrayed in the same way. The **audience** is the rest of the group. The **purpose** is for the other students to debate the points in each other's descriptions which are open to doubt or interpretation, such as the personal characteristics listed, and to reach some kind of consensus.

To build up the language of debate the teacher and the students can analyse spoken and written language which focuses on:

- negotiating
- expressing opinions
- giving personal reactions
- persuading
- making suggestions
- seeking opinions
- seeking agreement

and build up useful expressions. Alternatively students can be given lists from which they choose and use an increasing variety of phrases. The lists could look like the one opposite (see Appendix pp85 and 89 for German and Spanish versions).

Useful language phrases to structure what you say orally

1 • Ouverture – introduction

Alors …
J'ai choisi de présenter le thème de …
Le sujet de mon exposé est …
J'ai décidé de présenter le problème | de …
| qu'est …
Je voudrais parler de …
Mon exposé traite de. ..
Cette année, | j'ai fait des recherches sur …
| j'ai travaillé sur le thème de …
| je me suis penché sur …
| mon choix s'est porté sur …

2 • Poser un problème

Alors, voilà … comment parler de … ?
C'est un problème difficile auquel je vais
(essayer de) répondre le plus clairement
possible.
Tout d'abord concentrons-nous sur …
Dans un | premier temps …
| second temps …
Concentrons-nous d'abord sur …
Il faut d'abord considérer | …
| le fait que …

3 • Transition

Passons maintenant à …
Nous allons maintenant voir un deuxième
aspect du problème …
J'arrive maintenant à ma | deuxième partie
| troisième partie
… qui parle de …
J'ai choisi ensuite d'aborder le problème
de …
Il nous faut maintenant considérer …
Après avoir présenté … je vais maintenant
parler de …

4 • Insistance

Il est important de souligner que …
Il faut surtout tenir compte de …
J'attire votre attention sur …
Il faut insister sur le fait que …

5 • Exprimer ce qui n'est pas sûr

Il est probable que …
Il se peut que …
Il semblerait que …
Apparemment …
Il est possible que …
A première vue il semblerait que … mais …
Il n'est pas certain que …

6 • Exprimer ce qui est sûr

Il est | clair que …/indéniable que …
| évident que …
On peut affirmer que …
Il est sûr et certain que …

7 • Exprimer un point de vue personnel

A mon avis …
Je pense que …
Pour moi …
Personnellement, je suis d'avis que …
Mon opinion sur le sujet est …
Il me semble que …

8 • Attirer l'attention du lecteur

Notons que …
Il est intéressant de noter que …
J'attire votre attention sur …
Vous pouvez voir que …/On peut voir que …

9 • Conclusion

En conclusion, je voudrais dire …
Pour conclure …
Pour terminer cet exposé …
Finalement …

Since all these phrases and expressions are in **written** form and many are going to be used in **oral presentations** students should have recordings – made perhaps with the FLA – on cassette so that correct models of intonation and accurate pronunciation can be rehearsed.

A further extension of this practice is for students to include a number of these phrases when working with a partner. To ensure that this happens students elect a 'peer mentor' or *'type sympa'*. The role of the *'type sympa'* is to sit in on a pair or small group as they discuss a topic and to note which expressions are used during the activity. If none is used this should be pointed out and suggestions made where appropriate phrases could have been included. Strict 'peer mentors' have even been known to ask groups to do the presentation a second time so that phrases do feature!

Most advanced Specifications allow notes and prompts to be used in the oral examination. Using prompts is a skill which needs practice. Given the need to research topics on their own and, using some of the study skills outlined earlier, students should be encouraged to prepare at home or in school private study time a presentation to others based on notes, prompts, keywords as stipulated in the appropriate syllabus. If this is to be done in class to the rest of the group – a very appropriate audience if the topic is informative – Overhead Projector Transparencies (OHTs), handouts, pictures, PowerPoint, etc should be used. Such visual aids not only help create a clear framework, decided before the presentation itself and serving as an aide-mémoire, but, if photocopied, can provide a summary of key facts for the audience. If aids are going to be used it is important for all the written language to be accurate. A suggested process might be therefore for the draft to be:

- worked out with a partner; this is best if word-processed on screen with the partner working alongside, then;
- checked by FLA/teacher/student-teacher;
- corrected and put into a final form for the presentation;
- recorded during the presentation onto audio- or video-cassette.

An alternative preparatory stage might be for students to make a recording of their draft presentation on audiocassette. Teachers can then add their spoken comments onto the same cassette and, if necessary, advise students to make a second recording. This has the advantage that a record is kept by the student not only of the content and language used but of their pronunciation, intonation, etc which may either be appropriate and serve as a model for revision, or need improvement, with guidance on the cassette explaining how this may be achieved. If there are serious problems the students' needs can form the basis of a follow-up lesson or of a session with the FLA. Audio or videocassettes are also a useful basis for self-analysis and, if needs are identified, for further work with the FLA or the teacher.

It is clear from these comments that personal audiocassettes help students when they prepare oral work. They also provide an audio record of language to which students can listen for revision or to rehearse language not remembered accurately. It is recommended, therefore, that each student has his or her personal cassettes which include:

- audio texts recorded by the teacher from the radio, etc;

- audio recordings made by the student, monitored by the teacher or FLA, which are a record of new language – phrases rather than lists of nouns – thought to be re-usable;

- very short reconstructed passages based on an audio model (video clips are good for this) recorded by the students;

- examples, recorded by the students, of ways to present information/opinions, etc in preparation for the examination.

To develop writing skills

The list shown above serves the purpose of providing a range of language which can be used in **oral** and in **written** presentations. It is, however, unwise to use complete lists like this at an early stage in the advanced course. They appear daunting and, more significantly, the language is taken out of context. So, keeping this comprehensive version in reserve, a suggested approach would be to use limited written models which focus on and exemplify, one at a time, different kinds of language such as:

- the language of description;
- the language of publicity;
- the language of argumentation;

all three of which can include topic-specific vocabulary and expressions, etc.

Then, as has been exemplified when building up student confidence in oral presentations, go from the simple to the complex: from words > to sentences > to paragraphs > to whole texts.

Here are some examples:

At the word level

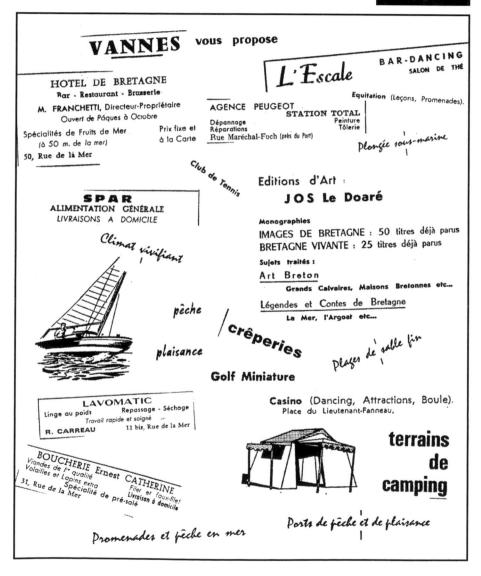

The task here might be to produce a similar page for a travel brochure based on the students' home town or, if they do not see this as sufficiently attractive, on a nearby town which they consider to be more interesting.

The language collected, mostly nouns, can be the basis for extension by:

■ qualifying some of the nouns with adjectives;

■ inventing simple phrases addressed to a potential visitor:
> *Si vous souhaitez acheter des ..., allez chez ...*
> *Si vous souhaitez faire de la natation, allez ...*
> *Pour ceux qui préfèrent des vacances actives Vannes vous propose ...*
> *Pour ceux qui préfèrent des vacances moins actives Vannes vous offre ...*
> *Pour ceux qui aiment se régaler au restaurant ... sont à votre disposition ...*

The language of advertising is easily found in Tourist Information Centres, local newspapers, etc.

Example 2

aint-Tropez ? Pyjamas. Dos nus. Boîtes à débardeurs truqués pour touristes riches. Deux cents autos de marque à partir de cinq heures, en travers du port. Cocktails, champagne sur les yachts à quai, et la nuit, sur le sable des petites criques, vous savez... »

Non, je ne sais pas. Je ne sais vraiment pas. Je connais l'autre Saint-Tropez. Il existe encore. Il existera toujours pour ceux qui se lèvent avec l'aube.

Quand mon golfe des Cannebiers dort encore, avant que son azur englouti ne remonte jusqu'à sa vague courte, j'atteins, à petit bruit de moteur et les roues cotonnées de poussière blanche, la ville qui s'éveille assez tard et je gagne le port, où bâille et s'étire quelqu'un de ces matelots de tartane, qui ont souvent des pieds charmants, nus, polis par l'eau de mer.

Rien ne bouge encore dans la rangée des yachts amarrés, qui naviguent peu. A cette heure, ils sont comme morts et ne me gênent pas. Derrière eux, les tartanes vides se balancent, trinquent mollement entre elles, avec un doux bruit de muids vides. Beaux yachts blancs, fins yachts noirs rehaussés d'or, yachts d'acajou couleur de Peaux-Rouges...

> COLETTE

Colette, *Prisons et paradis* © Librairie Arthème Fayard, 1932

In Colette's novel *Prisons et paradis* Saint-Tropez is described in an evocative way in which verbs initially do not feature – shown in the first paragraph of the text above. Students follow the model and describe a place they know in the same style, using no verbs.

At the sentence level

There are several ways to extend the content and form of sentences. These include:

■ making contrasts:
> *Maintenant je suis ... mais il y a un an j'étais ...*
> *Maintenant je suis ... mais il y a un mois j'étais ...*
> *Maintenant je suis ... mais il y a une semaine j'étais ...*
> *Maintenant je suis ... mais il y a un jour j'étais ...*
> *Maintenant je suis ... mais il y a une heure j'étais ...*

■ substituting words:
> *Vider les poubelles? C'est ce que j'aime le plus.*
> *Faire la vaisselle? C'est ce que je déteste le plus.*
> *Préparer les repas? C'est ce que j'aime le plus.*
> *Embrasser ma tante? C'est ce que je déteste le plus.*
> *Laver mon petit frère ...*

■ adding reasons and justifications:
> *J'étais triste parce que ...*

■ using a range of beginnings to add variety:
> *Une fois arrivée, elle ...*
> *Après un excellent déjeuner, Victor ...*
> *Ayant terminé la lettre, je ...*

■ including relative clauses:
> *La ville que je trouve très laide a néanmoins beaucoup de distractions ...*

At the paragraph level

The skill of writing paragraphs in the language can be developed by copying models from different types of text.

The description below written by La Bruyère has a clear structure. The reader's eye is taken around the grounds of the Château de Chantilly by the use of words like *ici, là, d'un côté ...*

Example 3

La Bruyère,
Les caractères
(describing the Château
de Chantilly)

VOYEZ, LUCILE, *ce morceau de terre, plus propre et plus orné que les autres terres qui lui sont contiguës : ici ce sont des compartiments mêlés d'eaux plates et d'eaux jaillissantes; là des allées en palissade qui n'ont pas de fin, et qui vous couvrent des vents du nord; d'un côté c'est un bois épais qui défend de tous les soleils, et d'un autre un beau point de vue. Plus bas, une Yvette ou un Lignon, qui couloit obscurément entre les saules et les peupliers, est devenu un canal qui est revêtu; ailleurs de longues et fraîches avenues se perdent dans la campagne, et annoncent la maison, qui est entourée d'eau. Vous récrierez-vous : « Quel jeu du hasard! combien de belles choses se sont rencontrées ensemble inopinément! » Non sans doute; vous direz au contraire : « Cela est bien imaginé et bien ordonné; il règne ici un bon goût et beaucoup d'intelligence. »*

A writing task based on this model might be:

Remarquez la structure de la description faite par La Bruyère:

- ici …
- là …
- d'un côté …
- et d'un autre …
- plus bas …
- ailleurs …

Faites une description d'un endroit que vous connaissez. Suivez la même structure.

The two examples which follow are ways in which personal descriptions can be extended. The emphasis on two features, the juxtaposition of contrasting statements, can be helpful to create structure **within** sentences. Discussion in class can explore ways of expressing all the thoughts described here but in a way which avoids the use of bullet points and therefore requires links **between** sentences.

Example 4

Situation familiale

Dans ma situation familiale, j'aime bien:
- l'argent de poche que l'on me donne
- j'ai le droit de sortir quand je veux
- les plats que cuisinent ma mère
- mon petit frère

Par contre, je n'aime pas :
- qu'on fouille dans mes affaires
- sortir le chien
- faire le ménage
- ma sœur (on se dispute tout le temps!)

MULLER Stéphanie

J'aime :
- que l'on m'aide pour faire mes devoirs
- faire des gâteaux
- quand mes parents vont au cinéma
- jouer de la guitare
- avoir des animaux
- être tranquille dans ma chambre

Le Née Julien
4ᵉ B

Je n'aime pas :
- débarrasser la table
- mon frère (ennuyant)
- aller faire les courses au supermarché
- prêter mes affaires (walkman)
- faire mon lit
- ranger ma chambre
- passer l'aspirateur

P

At the level of coherent text

The most demanding form of writing is coherent text. This writing skill needs to be developed. A simple beginning might be to start with a short text. Prévert's *Déjeuner du Matin* lends itself to the following treatment:

- cover text;
- reveal a line;
- decide key words after discussion;
- predict next part.

The complete poem, cut into lines, can then be reconstructed in any way which makes sense and which is grammatically correct. This is a revealing activity since it shows that new meaning can be created, either as sense or as non-sense, and grammatical coherence respected.

Other possible approaches are to:

- **make a text longer:**
  - add an ending to a story;
  - add a beginning to a story;
  - add adjectives, adverbs;
  - add sentences.

Try this game: from an initial sentence given by the teacher each student adds another one and passes the text on. The end product is then developed in class to produce a coherent text by making links between the separate parts.

- **make a text shorter:**
  - censor a story;
  - write a summary as continuous text or as notes.

- **reconstitute a text:**
  - an oral/written text is rebuilt by students.
  - example: 1 put together a recipe using markers of sequencing and instructing.
  - 2 teacher tells a story – students take notes – teacher illustrates coherence markers – students rewrite the story then compare versions (see Queneau: *Exercices de style*).

- **reform a text:**
  - a text is rewritten from another viewpoint or with different information.
  - example: 1 write a letter in answer to one received.
  - 2 edit a letter to convey different information; a useful task since a

letter format can be re-used once students have become familiar with the appropriate conventions.

- **interpret a text:**
  - students respond to a text in an affective or personal way (the language for this activity can be selected from the list shown above).

- **transfer media:**
  - spoken language from TV, video, film can be changed into a written version; reported speech requires a range of tenses which need constant practice!

A worked example

A way of progressing from the paragraph to coherent text is to start by developing something to write about – the ideas – and the language in which these can be expressed, then to look at ways of structuring the writing. Language links – *charnières* – can be integrated into what is written to provide further textual coherence. The following example is in French – see Appendix pp86 and 90–91 for German and Spanish versions.

Step 1: collecting language and ideas

À quoi bon les langues?

On dit que les langues sont utiles. Est-ce vrai? Voici des raisons données par des élèves anglais pour et contre l'apprentissage des langues. Êtes-vous plutôt pour ou contre? Lisez le texte qui suit.

Arguments pour l'étude d'une langue étrangère. L'étude d'une langue:	Arguments contre l'étude d'une langue étrangère:
• permet des contacts directs avec des étrangers ou dans votre pays ou dans le pays visité lors d'un voyage;	• tout le monde parle anglais;
• donne accès à une vision du monde, une culture et une civilisation;	• la plupart des étrangers que l'on rencontre en Angleterre veulent parler anglais;
• constitue une aide dans le monde du travail car de plus en plus d'emplois exigent la connaissance d'une langue étrangère.	• apprendre une langue étrangère est difficile; même après cinq ans peu de gens arrivent à communiquer dans le pays étranger.

Travaillez avec un(e) partenaire. Décidez quelles sont les raisons les plus importantes pour vous. Écrivez-les.

Step 2: adding language of opinion

Toujours avec votre partenaire choissisez des phrases dans cette liste. Suivez la structure.

1 • Présenter le thème

Le thème du jour est … , et j'aimerais le développer.
Premièrement …
Dernièrement, on a pu voir aux actualités, …
Tout d'abord/Nous aborderons …

2 • Poser un problème

On est de nouveau | face à …
confronté au problème de …

3 • Souligner ce qui est important

Il est vital que …
Il est très important de …
Rappelons que …
Il faut souligner que …
N'oublions surtout pas …

4 • Passer au point suivant

Nous examinerons maintenant …
Analysons maintenant …
Considérons à présent …

5 • Exprimer 'pas sûr'

Il est probable que …
Il n'est pas évident que …
Il se pourrait que …
Peut-être …

6 • Exprimer un point de vue personnel

Je pense/à mon avis/je crois que …
Selon moi/en ce qui me concerne …

7 • Attirer l'attention du lecteur

Insistons sur le fait que …
Très important …
J'attire votre attention sur le fait que …

8 • Exprimer ce qui est sûr/pas sûr …

Il est évident que …
Il est certain que …
Il est indéniable que …

9 • Comment conclure

Pour finir …
Finalement …
Pour conclure/en conclusion …
En somme/en définitive …
Donc/enfin/pour résumer/en résumé

Not only does the list provide language, it also shows ways to set out an argument. Further stylistic improvements can be made by adding a increasing range of *charnières* in written work. In French these include:

mais	d'ailleurs	au reste
et	du moins	autrement
car	néanmoins	de plus
aussi	puis	ensuite
ce qui, ce que	en revanche	ou
cependant	or	pour autant
d'autre part	pourtant	sinon
en effet	par ailleurs	toutefois
en outre	par contre	au surplus
encore	par conséquent	d'un autre côté
également	au contraire	de son côté

See Appendix pp87 and 91 for German and Spanish equivalents.

As always, writing collaboratively and discussing the writing process as it happens increases linguistic awareness and builds up confidence. This is a particularly successful strategy if a native speaker can be involved in a post-draft stage, when initial ideas have already been formulated but when accuracy, the choice of *le mot juste* and the use of linking phrases and *charnières* can be discussed and textual coherence enhanced.

Teachers will always have their preferred ways of encouraging writing of this kind. Most will have different kinds of 'writing frames' to encourage a sensitivity to structure. Many, too, devise ways to enable students to check their own written work. A systematic approach, elaborated over time, will start with:

- check solo/with a friend/FLA
  - looking at language: verb endings/tenses/spelling
  - looking at style: is it convincing/repetitive/varied?

Evaluation

Reward yourself!

It is important for students to see the merit of including some of the features outlined above in their own work. They should be encouraged to **reward themselves** by, for example, giving themselves points for useful phrases included. So that their readers (other students, the FLA, other teachers in the department, others in general) see why these points are awarded the student can highlight new words, phrases included, and words looked up, using different colours, e.g.

- *green for seen*
- *blue for new.*

Such a strategy helps develop and encourage critical evaluation and analysis.

Marking

Teachers always spend considerable time marking and providing feedback to students. It is worth discussing ways in which this benefits the student; what, for example, in the students' experience, helps improve future writing or speaking, and what does not. Given the time and care taken by teachers it is often surprising that the procedures they adopt are infrequently evaluated.

In order to learn from mistakes students need clear guidance on what to do when corrected work is returned, in terms of both content and language enhancement. They should be asked to analyse errors rather than merely look at corrected versions. A system of correction where numbers are used to denote the kind of error made, for example:

1   incorrect word order
2   incorrect tense
3   incorrect verb form, verb ending
4   incorrect spelling
5   incorrect gender
6   incorrect agreement
7   anglicism
8   word does not exist

may lead to greater and more detailed analysis. Targets, with a clear, unambiguous and limited focus, can be set as a result of an approach like this, which is often what individual learners need.

Using ICT for writing

A word processor is perhaps one of the greatest inventions ever in terms of facilitating the process of writing.

Encourage good practice in writing from an early stage through the use of writing frameworks – the teacher provides electronically a list of questions to which students respond in full sentences. The teacher's questions are then deleted, leaving a coherent passage of text, which the student can look to improve by inserting and deleting additonal vocabulary, such as conjunctions, adjectives and relative pronouns.

Use of Internet-based machine translator

There was a huge outcry from many language teachers as they discovered the Internet-based machine translator – Babelfish (http://babelfish.altavista.com/).

This allows a student to type in text in English and then select a language to translate into – the results are returned in seconds and there is little doubt that this is now a regular source of some students' coursework. However, it is far from perfect and most teachers would be able to spot when it has been used.

For example, translating a news article recently into French, German and Spanish – the name Mike Tyson was rendered as 'microphone' Tyson in all three languages!

Rather than attempting to hide this technology from students, it can serve as a wonderful tool for highlighting the sorts of errors that can occur in translation and be used to encourage sensible dictionary skills. Students can examine the text and analyse the reasons for the errors (Babelfish did not recognise that 'Mike' is a man's name), thereby improving their own skills in writing.

Tandem learning

Learning in tandem can be defined as a form of open learning, whereby two people with different native languages work together in pairs in order to:

- learn more about one another's character and culture;
- help one another in the improvement of their language skills;
- exchange additional knowledge on any topic.

Tandem language-learning takes place through authentic communication with a native speaker, who can correct and support the learner in their attempts to express themselves. Since each partner can speak a little of the other's language, there are opportunities to help each other through correcting errors and giving explanations. E-mail is an interesting form of communication as it tends to use a spoken, informal register in a written form – students seem to be less intimidated by this than by more formal essay or letter writing. For further information, see:

- www.slf.ruhr-uni-bochum.de/email/
- www.elok.com/rendezvous/

Essay writing

Students have used the 'forums' [sic] section of the site www.phosphore.com in developing writing skills for discursive essays. Typically, this can involve spending one lesson reading for gist on a particular topic. Students then analyse the comments on the site in more detail, organising the comments into 'for', 'against' and 'fact' sections. This can then be developed into an essay. As a final stage, students can e-mail their own comments to the site, providing a global audience for their contribution.

On-screen marking

Students prepare their work in a Microsoft Word document. The teacher marks it by highlighting errors and then using 'Insert > Comment' to highlight the nature of the error (verb tense, spelling, word order). The document is then saved and returned to the student, who then reviews and corrects the errors. This can lead to greater understanding of errors and a more critical approach to written work.

Another approach to this would be for students to write a piece of work and then make a checklist of all the things that they think could be possible errors (gender, verb form, spelling, etc.) They then use this checklist to mark a piece of work from another student (using the Insert Comment technique mentioned above). After marking the work, students amend their list of errors and then return to their own piece of work to correct their own mistakes, using their own checklist of common errors (from a NOF project undertaken by Esther Wrixon of St Mary Redcliffe and Temple School, Bristol).

Using ICT for speaking

While it is widely acknowledged that computers can assist with writing skills, as detailed above, there is little recognition of the support that can be gained for speaking skills.

Using MS PowerPoint for oral presentations

PowerPoint is part of the Microsoft Office suite and is used for giving presentations by displaying a slide onto a screen.

Source material: www.info13.com/pagnol/vie.html

Ask students to prepare materials for an oral presentation using PowerPoint slides. The bullet-points in PowerPoint act as 'prompts' while the student is speaking. Visual aids that can be added enhance the overall impact of the presentation, support the speaker and help to improve confidence.

Classroom idea: one student from the class is selected each week to present the week's news from the target language country to the other students, sourcing materials from the Internet. He or she does a five-minute oral presentation and prepares a one-page handout with key vocabulary, headings and snippets of stories for other students to read. These then form the basis of further discussion.

NB: This scenario could equally well be used on an OHT if PowerPoint and a data-projector are not available.

- Ensure speaking skills are developed for an audience and a purpose.
- Encourage students to prepare their own recordings on audio-cassette.
- Copy models of different types of text to extend writing skills.
- Help students evaluate and mark their own work and reward themselves.
- Use e-mail to develop native-speaker contacts.
- Use ICT to prompt oral presentations.

Grammatical accuracy

The priority for all teachers is to decide what their approach to grammar teaching is going to be. Once made the decision should be shared and discussed with the students. The key questions would seem to be:

1   Should students own and use a grammar book; if so, which one and how and when should it be used? Students need training in using a grammar book!

2   Should the teacher devise a systematic grammar course that is taught as such?

3   Should grammar be taught as it occurs in the teaching materials?

4   Should the teacher teach grammar as it is needed?

In all probability answers to these questions are:

1   Students should own and use a **common** grammar book. If all have the same book the teacher can illustrate how and when it can best be used. Decisions about which book to buy can be decided by the group after they have experimented with a few inspection copies.

2   The teacher will probably want to devise a systematic grammar course which relects both the requirements of the relevant A level Specification and students' needs. Students, too, seem to feel that grammar should be taught systematically and explicitly. There does appear to be a general feeling that grammar should always be taught in contexts which relate to different parts of the syllabus being followed.

3   In addition to a teacher's planned grammar course grammatical features are
& 4   normally explained as they arise. It is perhaps helpful for students if the materials are chosen to reflect at least some of the progression in the grammar

course and vice versa. This sequencing would also imply that teachers tackle grammar as and when it is needed.

Given the emphasis in all advanced Specifications on an explicit knowledge of grammar and its accurate use, an approach to grammar must be well integrated. However, planning a scheme of work is complex if students are, on the one hand, to explore isolated instances of particular grammatical features as they occur and, at the same time, understand how these form part of a wider, coherent whole. It is for this reason that starting exclusively from authentic texts which dictate to a degree what grammar will be identified is not as helpful as **starting from photographs, cartoons, drawings, paintings and purpose-written texts where the teacher is in control of the grammatical point to be considered.** This is the approach which is advocated here.

A further and important consideration is what terminology to use and what should be in the target language.

Where to start

It seems advisable to make systematic use of a range of **tenses** at the earliest opportunity and to encourage students to keep clear and accurate notes, preferably referenced to specific sections in their grammar book.

An approach might be to:

(i) **consolidate grammatical features** covered in GCSE. In the case of verbs, start by emphasising the use of the **infinitive.** This is infrequently understood and without a clear understanding of it the grammar book and the dictionary are of limited use.

(ii) **start from a carefully chosen visual prompt or some anecdote** written by the teacher or the FLA which will involve the use of a limited range of tenses; of most interest, both personal and cultural, are:

– personal accounts or confessions or descriptions of other teachers (tense potential: present, conditional, future – see example below);

– postcards of scenes from black and white films (excellent for the use of the imperfect tense);

– postcard reproductions of paintings by Picasso, Braque, Léger, Impressionists, cartoons by Sempé, etc.

Tense potential: what **is** he/she thinking?
what **might have happened** before the event portrayed?
what **might happen next?**
the character **is** sad/happy because a relative **has just ...**
the violin and the newspaper belong to a man who **is** strange because he **reads ...**

(iii) **develop grammatical awareness by encouraging pattern spotting;** start the use of **terminology in the target language** to categorise the grammatical features found and, if the focus is on verbs, go back to the infinitive before exploring tense formation or the use of other tenses.

(iv) **move to grammatical categorisation** and add illustrations or examples **in context.**

What does this mean for the students' study skills?

It is important for students to have a system in place for recording what they have learnt in an easily accessible and adaptable format, as has been advocated earlier. A system must allow for notes to be added and information to be stored in categories such as:

Theme- or topic-based

Use the topic lists from the appropriate examinations board – the media, advertising, the arts, daily life, food and drink, etc and

- talk about what will happen;
- talk about what would happen if ...;
- talk about what has happened;
- talk about what used to happen, or was happening;
- talk about what is happening, or happens all the time;

and (chosen as appropriate)

- make comparisons;
- use quantifiers *très, assez, beaucoup*
sehr, besonders, kaum, recht, wenig
muy, bastante, poco, mucho;

* use interrogative adjectives   *quel?, quelle?*
                                      welcher?
                                      ¿cuánto?, ¿qué?.

(These are taken from the QCA prescribed grammar and syntax lists shown in all advanced Specifications.)

Record a rule as a grammar note

Organise this on postcards (see below) – and record when the note was written (and when re-read and used as part of a regular review of what has been done over time).

Refer to a published grammar reference book

Use one common to and owned by all students, and note the relevant page.

If there is such a system in place encourage the students to set their own learning targets on individual self-help or planning sheets in a weekly, timetabled format (an example of which was shown in Chapter 1, p11). This should be related to a teacher's weekly/termly grammar progression/content guide.

Students' use of their grammar notes

To help students memorise and learn grammar notes these should be contextualised; such a strategy is designed to illustrate how the grammatical feature – in this example, tenses – can be used. It also shows how common tasks such as talking about oneself can be developed both linguistically and as a theme.

In the notes written on a postcard (see below) an English translation of the verbs is included to clarify meaning. Since some students do not know with any kind of confidence what tenses in the other language mean this is often considered **by them** to be not only helpful but necessary! Patterns of verb endings are shown in colour (or by some other means) and markers, such as *maintenant, à l'avenir,* are added to reinforce the relationship, where it exists, between time and the appropriate use of tenses.

A teacher's termly grammar guide to show what will be covered might look like this example; these are suggestions for French from a local school for the first term.

LA GRAMMAIRE: septembre–décembre

- les temps: la formation du présent, du passé composé, de l'imparfait et du futur
- l'impératif
- la négation
- les genres
- les adjectifs
- les adjectifs possessifs
- les pronoms relatifs
- les pronoms directs/indirects
- tout, toute, tous, toutes
- ce, cet, cette, ces
- depuis

A glance at the syllabus requirements shown in the advanced Specifications does emphasise the need to extend quite quickly the students' range of grammatical competence. Some texts, while preserving the prime function which is to provide interesting content, do often have grammar features which lend themselves to effective categorisation.

In summary

To help students help themselves teachers can set tasks which require students to:

- work from texts and highlight known/unknown t enses/grammatical features;
- complete regular grammar-based tasks, which keep, as far as possible, meaning as an important feature;
- collect language and learn examples and rules by heart in the target language;
- review progress weekly and set limited personal targets.

Grammar and ICT

Some of the ideas already covered will help to develop grammatical comprehension and usage, but there are some additional tools which can focus on grammar structures.

The teacher uses PowerPoint for presentation/reinforcement of grammar

The way in which slides can be animated in PowerPoint allows the teacher to reveal and move text around the screen. Use of colour and pictures can also enhance the impact of this type of presentation, which can appeal to many different learning styles.

Example: when teaching the subjunctive, the teacher can bring up the stem of the verb, add endings and drop appropriate words in front of the subjunctive to illustrate how it is used.

On-line grammar tests

There are many on-line sites to help students test and extend their grammar. These are generally developed and run by enthusiastic teachers on their own homepages and so they can change regularly. In order to locate these, run a search for 'on-line grammar Spanish' in, for example, www.google.com. There will be many sites returned. You could even ask students to locate and test these and compile a list of the best to be added to the school's Intranet or produced as a list.

Developing grammar tests

As a teacher, you may like to look at exploiting Internet tools which allow teachers to develop their own on-line resources – or again, get the students to develop these and try them out on each other. Try:

- QUIA (www.quia.com) – develop quizzes on-line for use on-line;

- HOT POTATOES (http://web.uvic.ca/hrd/halfbaked) – download software to develop quizzes off-line;

- the CASTLE toolkit (www.le.ac.uk/cc/ltg/castle/) – develop quizzes to be used on-line.

Older software

There was a lot of software developed at an early stage in computer-assisted language learning where students were required to select and type in the correct form of a word – typically completing 20–100 questions and then getting a mark. This has affectionately come to be known as *drill and kill* as it can be quite boring. However, there are a number of students who will respond well to, and even enjoy, this type of repetition. It is certainly less boring than simply trying to commit words to memory and the one-on-one interaction the computer can offer does help to focus students' attention.

key points

- Encourage students to keep clear and accurate grammar notes.
- Develop recording formats, e.g. theme- or topic-based, where language can be categorised.
- Contextualise grammar with regular tasks.
- Exploit the Internet for ready-made, on-line grammar tests or to customise.
- Set targets and review progress weekly.

Exploring literary texts

Ways in – general

A literary text is frequently seen as a daunting prospect because the language is often complex and the content new and challenging. Students can, however, be led into texts in a gradual way to retain their confidence. There are several preparatory activities they can undertake beforehand. These include:

- researching from source material provided (which can often include extracts from the main text) and compiling information sheets on:
  - the author
  - the historical background
  - the appropriate social context
  - the region, etc
  using:
  - short texts (1/2 pages)
  - photos
  - video extracts
  - film extracts
  - travel brochures
  - historical accounts
  - own notes and summaries.

- planning for outcomes which include:
  - mini talks (student to student)
  - mini information packs.

Students frequently report how beneficial they find working collaboratively on joint projects. This is a potentially useful context, which, if supported by the teacher, FLA or even e-mail partner in the target country, can be a source of interesting and potentially useful material which they, not the teacher, have collected and annotated.

Ways in – to specific set texts

When the preparatory work has been completed students can be encouraged to work first on 'colourful' extracts, often treated in the same way that they would any short reading text. These can be used to highlight key ideas which will be developed later as the longer text is read and discussed. Such themes need, however, to be launched in modest ways so that the students are kept interested. When longer parts of the text have been read students can be encouraged to **choose extracts** and treat them in a number of different ways. They can:

■ act them out, using scripts based on a dialogue in a novel or parts in a play;

■ write a short résumé or a newspaper report of an event which is discussed by the rest of the group for its accuracy of information, omissions, appropriate or inappropriate emphases, etc;

■ describe as a spoken activity what they would do if they were in one of the situations described in the text;

■ work on a theme in the book, e.g. the theme of *solitude* cued by:
  – songs (Moustaki)
  – poems
  – extracts from Camus' *L'Étranger.*

If students are given the responsibility for the choice of content and subject matter their response is normally positive and committed. The selection of appropriate extracts, as well as the work based on them, not only focuses on content and ideas but is beneficial in developing language within the context of the set text; it also necessitates detailed reading so that key passages are well chosen.

With text in hand

There is a range of other possible activities which can be offered to students. These include:

■ devising interviews with students either being characters in a play or a novel, or between members of the class and a character in the play or novel;

- making up endings and discussing why these might or might not work;

- writing a letter from one character in a play or novel to another;

- devising a quiz based on quotations from the set text – *Did they really say that? True or false?;*

- in groups and with different extracts from different texts finding examples of, e.g. symbolism, striking characterisation, evocative description and then pooling the results for the class;

- producing a diagram of a story/theme/characterisation over time;

- 'adopting a character' and justifying the choice made;

- writing a short review from a given standpoint, e.g. from a feminist/royal/ Catholic/young child's, etc, viewpoint;

- summarising in (150) words pages 00 to 00.

Addendum: some examples of student tasks

Approaches to a text

- Cover whole text.
- Reveal a line of the text.
- Decide key words after discussion.
- Predict next part.

Approaches to a photo + text (e.g. newspaper article with accompanying photo)

Work as a class or in groups.

- Look at the photo only.
  - What is it about?
  - How do you know?
  - Why?

- What do you think the article will be about?
  - What vocab is likely to be used?

- Now read the text:
  - identify keywords/phrases;
  - ask the teacher who/why/what/where questions;
  - write up favourite phrases;
  - without looking try to reconstitute the text from memory;
  - make it personal;
  - imagine you were there;
  - debate the issues;
  - write a diary/notes;
  - make a presentation.

Approaches to using photos, text, headlines, video clips ...

- Practise language of conjecture.

Partner A asks:	Partner B uses language of conjecture:
c'est qui?	*il semble que ...*
c'est où?	*c'est peut-être ...*
c'est quand?	*il a l'air ...*

- Practise language of emotional reactions.
  With a partner list all the words you can use to react to the photo, headline, etc:
  incroyable, effrayant, choquant, violent ...

Then decide what language you need to develop.

Attacking a short text

Solo	1	read it;
	2	turn it over – write down any words remembered;
	3	re-read it;
	4	turn it over – write down phrases, verbs, infinitives, etc remembered;
	5	re-read it;
	6	write down all words not known;
With a partner	7	compare your lists with someone else's;
	8	agree on what the text is all about;
	9	turn it over;
	10	write an agreed version.

The Internet is a tremendous boon to the study of literary texts. As literature is something that people enjoy as a hobby, there are many Homepages which feature information about literary works and their authors. As mentioned in Chapter 2, learning to search for materials relating to topics at A level can greatly enhance a student's study in that area.

You may like to think about the following, all of which have been mentioned in earlier Chapters:

- Researching the work on the Internet;
- Discussing the work via e-mail with a correspondent in the target-language country;
- Using PowerPoint to give an oral presentation;
- Using a word processor to play games with a text – re-ordering, inserting, deleting, completing an unfinished text.

Oral presentation 1

In a role play select from Module 2 – Aspects of Society – information to give to a visitor. It should include:

1 facts and information
2 advice
3 explanations
4 opinions.

Present these in an organised way. Your teacher/FLA/student partner will play the part of the visitor.

Oral presentation 2

Present a topic from Module 1 – Young People Today.

To help remember the content you may use:

- maps
- diagrams
- statistics
- pictures
- key points on card.

NB: the conditions vary between examination boards:
– 5–10 key points allowed (Edexcel)
– 4 headings allowed which are given to the examiner (OCR)

The presentation should include:

1. an introduction – what your presentation is about;
2. first aspects;
3. next aspects;
4. key ideas for you;
5. personal opinion:
   – what you are not sure about;
   – what you are sure about;
6. conclusion.

Oral presentation 3: talking about yourself, possible holiday or part-time jobs

Look at the advertisements below and:

1. build up your vocabulary to talk about yourself.
2. use your tenses to say: – what job you do now to earn money
   – what you would like to do and why.
3. Justify your choice.

Use the texts below to decide:

- what is useful vocabulary for you;
- what phrases you can re-use;
- what tenses/verbs you need.

Quel boulot choisir?

La BONNE FOURCHETTE
recherche aide-cuisinier, samedi,
dimanche, midi et soir. 375 F par
jour. Téléphonez à M. Alphonse à
la BONNE FOURCHETTE.

Vous avez entre 16 et 18 ans? Le *Salon*
Alexandre vous propose de vous joindre à son
équipe prestigieuse de coiffeurs hommes/femmes
pour leur donner un coup de main le weekend.
Pas de qualifications requises. Pourboires
intéressants. **SALON UNISEX**

Décrivez votre candidat idéal pour chaque emploi:

Exemple:
il/elle aimerait …
il/elle ferait …
il/elle porterait …
il/elle serait …
il/elle choisirait …
il/elle comprendrait …
il/elle parlerait …

Lesquels des emplois vous intéressent-ils? Donnez les raisons de votre choix:

Moi, j'aimerais …
    je ferais …
    je porterais …
    je serais …
parce que …
    je choisirais …
    je comprendrais …
    je parlerais …

FLORIBEL s'aggrandit. Un vendeur ou une vendeuse serait bienvenu les jours de marché, mercredi, samedi et dimanche matin. Passez voir Mme Rose, Place du Petit Marché mercredi après-midi.

Le Centre Aéré Jules Vernes recherche pour sa garderie du mercredi après-midi **Moniteur ou Monitrice** aimant le contact avec les petits enfants de 3 à 5 ans. 50F de l'heure. S'adresser au Centre Aéré, rue Gambetta

600F la semaine MOTO 2000 demande aide mécanicien le mercredi après-midi et le samedi toute la journée. N'hésitez pas à nous contacter même si vous n'avez aucune expérience.

M. et Mme de la Ginestière aimeraient confier leur adorable pékinois Chochotte à une personne de confiance le weekend pendant le mois d'avril. Rémunération intéressante si références satisfaisantes. Contactez le plus rapidement pour entretien préliminaire.

key points

- Begin by researching the background and context of literary texts.
- Encourage students to work together and choose appropriate texts.
- Plan a variety of approaches and outcomes.
- Devise activities practising all four skills in pairs, groups and solo.
- Use the Internet to discuss the work being studied with native speakers.

Bibliography

Grenfell M (ed), *Reflections on reading: From GCSE to A level* (CILT, 1995)

Grenfell M and V Harris, *Modern languages and learning strategies in theory and practice* (Routledge, 1999)

Littlewood W (ed), *Developing modern language skills for GCSE* (Nelson, 1989)

Queneau R, *Exercices de style* (Editions Flammarion, 1949)

Shaw G (ed), *Aiming high 2: Straight A's* (CILT, 2000)

Websites

Autonomy and Independence in Language Learning: http://ec.hku.hk/autonomy/

Lingu@NET-forum: see p92 for further information.

Partner-finding websites
- Eloquence runs a penfriend service called 'Rendez Vous': www.elok.com/rendezvous/
- Windows on the World – Central Bureau: www.wotw.org.uk
- E-pals – in French, Spanish, German and Portuguese: www.epals.com
- Tandem Learning network: www.slf.ruhr-uni-bochum.de/email/idxeng00.html

Appendix 1

German examples

Chapter 4, p50

Stellen Sie sich vor, indem Sie die folgenden Sätze ergänzen:

Ich heisse …
Ich bin … Jahre alt.
Ich wohne in …
Zu meiner Familie gehören …
Jeden Tag   stehe ich um … auf
              frühstücke ich …
              fahre ich mit dem Auto zur die Schule …
Abends   esse ich …
              sehe ich fern …
              gehe ich um … ins Bett.
Am Wochenende …
Während der grossen Sommerferien …

Chapter 4, pp50–51

Beschreiben Sie, wie Sie sind

 Schreiben und ergänzen Sie diesen Satz ‚Ich bin nicht … aber ich bin …' indem Sie zwei Adjektive von der folgenden Liste wählen:

nervös	ungeduldig	arbeitsam
intelligent	liebenswert	nett
gesellig	dynamisch	sportlich
humorvoll	amüsant	verständnisvoll
schwierig	tüchtig	faul
mitteilsam	schüchtern	offen

2 Bilden Sie jetzt einen vollständigen Satz mit Hilfe der folgenden Wörter, wenn möglich, und ergänzen Sie Ihre persönliche Beschreibung.
Beispiel: Ich bin nicht intelligent, aber ich bin ziemlich arbeitsam.

> nicht sehr
> manchmal   ein wenig
>   wirklich
> ziemlich   sehr

3 Fahren Sie mit der Beschreibung fort; fügen Sie diesen Satz dort ein, wo er am besten hinpasst:

denn ich bin ... (schüchtern, ordentlich – es liegt bei Ihnen, das richtige Wort zu wählen).

Chapter 4, p53

Useful language phrases to structure what you say orally

1 • Zu Anfang

Mein Thema beschäftigt sich mit ...
Ich versuche das folgende Thema/die folgende Problematik näher zu erklären/zu erläutern
Ich möchte der folgenden Frage auf den Grund gehen
Ich möchte mich auf diesen Aspekt konzentrieren
Zuerst möchte ich einen Überblick über das Thema geben, später werde ich auf einzelne Fragen eingehen

2 • Um das Thema zu wechseln/die Aufmerksamkeit auf ... zu lenken

Auf der einen Seite - auf der anderen Seite ...
Ein anderes Problem dabei ist ...
Jetzt möchte ich auf eine andere Frage eingehen ...
Ich möchte einen anderen Aspekt ansprechen
Von einer anderen Seite betrachtet ...
Dabei muss berücksichtigt werden, dass ...

3 • Darauf bestehen

Ich möchte die Tatsache betonen, dass ...
Ich lege besonderen Wert auf ...
Es ist eindeutig, dass ...
Man kann keinesfalls behaupten, dass ...

4 • Was (nicht) sicher ist

Es kann nicht eindeutig behauptet werden, dass
Es ist nicht sicher, dass/ob ...
Es ist sicher, dass ...
Es kann behauptet werden ...
Die Schwierigkeit liegt in ...

5 • Zum Abschluss

Um zum Ende zu kommen
Ich möchte mein Referat damit abschliessen, dass ..
In einer abschließenden Bemerkung, möchte ich ...

Chapter 4, p62

Wozu sind Fremdsprachen gut?

Man sagt, dass Sprachen nützlich sind. Stimmt das? Im folgenden argumentieren englische Schüler und Schülerinnen für und gegen das Lernen von Sprachen. Sind Sie eher dafür oder dagegen? Lesen Sie den folgenden Text.

Argumente für das Studium einer Fremdsprache; es:	Argumente gegen das Studium einer Fremdsprache:
• ermöglicht unmittelbaren Kontakt zu Ausländern, entweder im eigenen Land oder beim Besuch im Ausland • vermittelt Zugang zu einer unterschiedlichen Weltanschauung, einer anderen Kultur und Zivilisation • hilft im Berufsleben, da für immer mehr Arbeitsstellen die Kenntnis einer Fremdsprache erforderlich ist.	• jederman spricht Englisch • die meisten Ausländer, denen man in England begegnet, wollen Englisch sprechen • das Lernen einer Fremdsprache ist schwierig; selbst nach fünf Jahren gelingt es wenigen Leuten, sich im fremden Land zu verständigen.

Arbeiten Sie mit einem Partner/einer Partnerin zusammen. Entscheiden Sie, welche Argumente für Sie am wichtigsten sind. Schreiben Sie sie auf.

Chapter 4, p63

Wählen Sie, ebenfalls mit Ihrem Partner/Ihrer Partnerin, Ausdrücke von der folgenden Liste. Folgen Sie der angegebenen Reihenfolge.

1 • Führen Sie das Thema ein

Das Thema des Tages ist ..., und ich möchte es weiter entwickeln.
Erstens ...
Zum Schluss kann man aus den Tatsachen ersehen ...
Zunächst/Wir werden ... angehen

2 • Weisen Sie auf ein Problem hin:

Man steht von neuem einem Problem gegenüber.

3 • Unterstreichen Sie, worauf es ankommt

Es ist unbedingt notwendig, dass ...
Es ist sehr wichtig, dass ...
Lassen Sie uns in Erinnerung rufen, dass ...
Man muss unterstreichen, dass ...
Vor allem dürfen wir nicht vergessen, dass ...

4 • Gehen Sie zum nächsten Punkt über

Wir werden jetzt ... näher betrachten.
Lassen Sie uns jetzt ... kritisch untersuchen.
Lassen Sie uns zunächst einmal ... erwägen.

P

5 • Bringen Sie zum Ausdruck, was ‚nicht sicher' ist:

Es ist wahrscheinlich, dass …
Es ist nicht offensichtlich, dass (ob) …
Es könnte sein, dass …
Vielleicht …

6 • Drücken Sie eine persönliche Meinung aus

Ich meine/meiner Meinung nach/ich glaube, dass …
Meiner Ansicht nach/was mich betrifft, so …

7• Erregen Sie die Aufmerksamkeit der Leser

Lassen Sie uns auf der Tatsache bestehen, dass …

Sehr wichtig, …
Ich möchte Ihre Aufmerksamkeit auf die Tatsache lenken, dass …

8 • Bringen Sie zum Ausdruck, was sicher/nicht sicher ist …

Es ist offensichtlich, dass …
Es ist sicher, dass …
Es kann nicht geleugnet werden, dass …

9 • So beschliessen Sie das Thema

Um zum Ende zu kommen …
Schliesslich …
Zum Abschluss
Also/endlich/zusammenfassend/um zusammenzufassen

Chapter 4, p64

aber	übrigens	letztlich
und	wenigstens	sonst
denn	nichtsdestoweniger	darüber hinaus
auch	dann	und dann
was	andererseits	oder
unterdessen	nun	soweit
auf der anderen Seite	dennoch	andernfalls
tatsächlich	weiterhin	gleichwohl
ausserdem	im Gegensatz	im übrigen
noch	folglich	in anderer Hinsicht
gleicherweise	im Gegenteil	seinerseits

Appendix 2
Spanish examples

Chapter 4, p50

Empieza tu presentación con estas expresiones. No te olvides de terminarlas primero.

Me llamo …
Tengo … años.
Vivo en …
En mi familia hay … personas.
Cada día   me levanto a las …
              desayuno …
              voy al colegio en …
Por la tarde   ceno …
              veo la tele …
              me acuesto …
El fin de semana suelo …
Durante las vacaciones de verano, me gusta …

Chapter 4, pp50–51

Describe tu carácter

1 Tienes que completar esta frase: 'No soy …, pero sí soy …' Para hacerlo, utiliza los adjetivos de la lista siguiente:

nervioso/a	impaciente	trabajador/a
inteligente	simpático/a	dinámico/a
deportivo/a	cómico/a	divertido/a
difícil	organizado/a	tímido/a
valiente	abierto/a	activo/a

| 2 | Después tienes que añadir a la frase una de estas expresiones. *Ejemplo: No soy organizado pero soy bastante trabajador.* |

algunas veces
no muy
bastante
muy
un poco

| 3 | Sigue con la descripción, añadiendo lo siguiente: |

porque soy una persona muy .... (con un adjetivo más, por ejemplo activa).

Chapter 4, p53

Useful language phrases to structure what you say orally

1 • Introducción

bueno, ...
he escogido hablar de ...
el tema de mi presentación es ...
he decidido presentar un tema que ...
quisiera hablar de ...
mi presentación trata de ...
este año | he trabajado sobre el tema de ...
he investigado el tema de ...
me he concentrado en ...
he querido estudiar ...

2 • Presentar un tema

es una cuestión difícil, que voy a tratar en reve.
para empezar, nos vamos a concentrar en ...
en primer lugar ...
hay que tener en cuenta el hecho de que ...

3 • Cambiar de tema

vamos a pasar al tema de ...
ahora vamos a ver un segundo elemento de
este problema.
después quiero abordar otro aspecto del tema.
después de presentar ... , quiero pasar a
hablar de ...
ahora tenemos que considerar que ...

4 • Insistir en algo

es importante notar que ...
sobretodo hay que tener en cuenta que ...
es importante no olvidar que ...

5 • Expresar dudas

es probable que ...
se puede que ...
parece que ...
por lo que parece, ...
es posible que
a primera vista parece que ...
no está claro si ...

6 • Cuando no hay dudas

está claro que ...
es obvio que ...
no se puede negar que ...
podemos estar seguros que ...
sin lugar a duda, ...

7 • Expresar un punto de vista personal

en mi opinión ...
creo que ...
para mí, ...
personalmente, ...
mi opinión sobre esto es que ...
me parece que ...

8 • Atraer la atención de tu público

es interesante comentar que …
se puede ver que …
si prestamos atención a …

9 • Conclusión

para terminar, quisiera comentar que …
a final de cuentas, …
al fin y al cabo, …
finalmente, …

Chapter 4, p62

¿Para qué sirve estudiar idiomas?

Se dice que los idiomas son útiles, pero ¿es verdad? Aquí tienes algunas razones presentadas por unos alumnos ingleses a favor y en contra de aprender idiomas extranjeros.

Argumentos a favor el estudio de un idioma:
- te deja hacer contactos directos con extranjeros, o en tu país o en el país donde estás de viaje;
- te deja entrar en otra visión del mundo, otra cultura y otra civilización;
- te proporciona un apoyo en el mundo del trabajo, porque cada vez más trabajos exigen el conocimiento de una lengua extranjera.

Argumentos en contra:
- todo el mundo habla inglés;
- casi todos los extranjeros que vienen a Inglaterra quieren practicar el inglés;
- aprender un idioma extranjero es difícil; aun después de cinco años, poca gente llega a comunicarse bien en un país extranjero.

Trabaja con otro alumno/otra alumna. Buscad las razones más importantes y, después, escribidlas.